The High-Functioning Marriage

How to Make Your Marriage Flourish

A FAMILY LIFE HANDBOOK - VOLUME 2

MANNIE SAMUELSEN AZENDA
Author of *Dating Etiquette for Singles*

The High-Functioning Marriage
Copyright © 2022 by Mannie Samuelsen Azenda

The names, characters, places, and incidents portrayed in this book are fictitious. No identification with actual persons (living or dead) and places is intended or should be inferred.

Scriptures taken from New King James Version (NKJV) unless otherwise stated. NKJV Copyright 1982 by Thomas Nelson. Used by permission. All rights reserved.

All rights reserved. No part of this publication may be reproduced, distributed, or transmitted in any form or by any means, including photocopying, recording, or other electronic or mechanical methods, without the prior written permission of the author, except in the case of brief quotations embodied in critical reviews and certain other non-commercial uses permitted by copyright law.

Tellwell Talent
www.tellwell.ca

ISBN
978-0-2288-7339-6 (Hardcover)
978-0-2288-7337-2 (Paperback)
978-0-2288-7338-9 (eBook)

TABLE OF CONTENTS

Dedication vii
Acknowledgements ix
Endorsements xi
Preface xiii

Subtle Marriage Lubricants 1

Chapter 1: The Power of Agreement 5
Chapter 2: The Therapeutic Power of Apology 23
Chapter 3: Let your Spouse be Enough 33
Chapter 4: The Power of a Wise Counsel 45

Marital Responsibilities for Husbands 53

Chapter 5: The Husband's unconditional love for his Wife ... 57
Chapter 6: Nourish, Cherish, and Care for Your Wife 71

Figure I: Love: Nourish, Cherish and Care Interconnection ... 71

Chapter 7: Provide Leadership to Your Wife 85

Marital Responsibilities of Wives 97

Chapter 8: Wife's Submission To Her Husband 101
Chapter 9: Wife's Cheerleading Her Husband 123

Areas of Mutual Responsibility 129

Chapter 10: Mutual Marital Responsibilities 133
Chapter 11: Respect.. 141
Chapter 12: Prioritization 153
Chapter 13: Support.. 167
Chapter 14: Care, Provision, and Protection 177
Chapter 15: Partnership.. 185
Chapter 16: Sexual Intimacy 199
Chapter 17: Bequeathing Legacies 217

The Anatomy of a Failed Marriage 235

Chapter 18: Biblical Position on Divorce 239
Chapter 19: The Impact of Divorce on the Society 255
Chapter 20: The Impact of Fatherlessness on Children 267

Table I – Mother and Father's Parental Roles.................. 268

Figure II: Father's Responsibility Cycle 271

Chapter 21: Emotional and Psychological Impact of
              Divorce... 283
Chapter 22: When Divorce Becomes the only Option...... 293

There is Hope and a Future 299

Chapter 23: Hope for the Divorced 303
Chapter 24: Hope for the Fatherless Child 315

About the Author.. 336

List of Tables

Table I – Mother and Father's Parental Roles......................268

List of Figures

Figure I: Love: Nourish, Cherish and Care Interconnection...71

Figure II: Father's Responsibility Cycle..............................271

DEDICATION

I dedicate this book to the loving memory of my dad, Samuel Azenda Abiagi, who mentored me and helped me become the person I am today. Dad, you taught me what it means to serve God. You also taught me the value of hard work, strong moral values, and humility. As well, I learned how to be a husband and a dad just by watching you. You truly were the epitome of an exemplary father.

I also dedicate this book to the evergreen memory of my mom, Hannah K. Azenda. Your insight, foresight, and wisdom remain unparalleled. I am grateful for your prayers that only a very special mom like you could have prayed. You were simply the best!

Finally, I dedicate this book to the memory my grandma, Ruth Ashide Abiagi, the linchpin that held the family together. You worked tirelessly and sacrificed for the well-being of our family. Your entrepreneurial spirit and energy were second to none.

ACKNOWLEDGEMENTS

A special thanks to my wife and friend, Dr. Chino Azenda, for her dedication and relentless support in my life and ministry. Honey, you're truly the best!

I owe my children a debt of gratitude for painstakingly going through the manuscript and providing invaluable feedback.

I am deeply grateful to the following important individuals who through careful review of the manuscript, prayers, encouragement, and support have contributed to this book's publication: Pastor Helen Burns, Ed and Carol Huculak, Stella Jonah, Pastor Matthew Uponi, Joe and Pat Nwaroh, Pastor Anayo Onwuka, Henry and Maureen Oluedo.

ENDORSEMENTS

After reading, "A Family Life Handbook - Volume 2", it is clear to me that Pastor Mannie has a great passion to see marriages thrive. He draws on his experience as a pastor and counsellor along with his study of God's Word as the foundation for the principles he outlines in this book. I am inspired by his dedication and commitment to serve marriages and families as this book is clearly a labour of love to guide, instruct and encourage readers as they build their lives on the wisdom of the Word of God.

- Helen Burns
Co-Founder and Teaching Pastor,
Relate Church, Surrey,
British Columbia, Canada.

A captivating and inspiring book! I have to admit that Samuelsen is a brilliant writer with a plethora of marriage-related experience and knowledge. I'm incredibly thrilled to have the opportunity to edit and proofread "The High-Functioning Marriage." He did a phenomenal job of conveying the significance of a high-functioning marriage and how to achieve one. The High-Functioning Marriage is fully packed with nuggets of advice, real-life marital experiences, and powerful prayer points. I highly recommend singles and couples pick up a copy, as it would definitely transform their lives.

-Wendy Joe

A must read book for everyone who is contemplating marriage. Learn what the advantages are to being married, hint: even your health is affected. This is an honest manual to help you learn and live a happy married life.

-Edward J. Huculak,
former Publisher of the Winnipeg Sun;
former Publisher/Director of Sales of The Calgary Sun;
Wedding Officiant.

PREFACE

Marriage is a magnificent, highly desirable, and exciting undertaking. It's such a beautiful undertaking that can positively change one's status in life for good. Anyone who falls in love and nurtures the relationship into a marriage has enlisted in a desirous and honorable institution. It's honorable and desirous because almost every human being, regardless of where they live on the face of the earth, desires to enlist in this institution called marriage. While not everyone will marry in their lifetime, nearly everyone desires to do so. Also, immediate families and society generally expect people to get married at some stage in their lives. Furthermore, the desirability of marriage is evident in how even those who have previously experienced a failed marriage have often looked forward to trying it again and again.

Rightly or not, an assumed aura of maturity and responsibility goes with a married person. And that aura is often lacking or assumed to be lacking when a person remains unmarried beyond a certain stage in their life. That's part of why marriage is such an important milestone when it is achieved, tends to enhance one's status as well as how others perceive them.

However, as I've helped many couples in different cultures navigate their conflicts and differences, some common patterns and viewpoints have become evident in most cases. These patterns have formed the inspiration behind the writing of this book. I am writing it with a strong belief that the book would help couples in many parts of the world who will probably never hear me speak or see me in person to have this as a reference handbook in their homes.

The patterns and viewpoints I've observed include the following:

Lack of understanding of what marriage is

This may sound like a fairy tale to many, but anyone involved in marriage therapy or counseling probably knows how real this issue is. Part of the reason may be that most people grow up and naturally look forward to when they will get married. However, it doesn't cross their mind that they should take the time and understand what marriage is all about. For many, their understanding is limited to the oversimplified version of marriage, which is for two people to love themselves enough to agree to live together as husband and wife. Some of these people have no idea what the origin or purpose of marriage is or why it is such a desirable thing to do for most people. If you feel this describes your situation, let me refer you to my prior book, *Dating Etiquette for Singles,* which is a good book that'll fill those gaps in your understanding of what marriage is.

Lack of understanding of one's marital responsibilities

Every job has its own responsibilities. That's why when you're newly hired for a role in a company, your manager will help you to understand what your responsibilities are. Your job responsibilities will also help you understand what is being expected of you. For this reason, one is more likely to be successful in their job if they have a clear understanding of the responsibilities of the job they are hired to do. The same is true of marriage. Being a spouse is a serious job that comes with responsibilities and expectations. You'll be a great spouse if you can make the required effort to understand and perform your responsibilities in your marriage.

Lack of appreciation of the need to work on one's marriage

Marriage demands hard work. And a marriage that is going to thrive will require a lot of hard work. In fact, the quality of your marriage is directly correlated to the intentionality and quality of work you're willing to put into it. Many couples simply assume that a good and high-functioning marriage just happens. This mistake of thinking that a good marriage just happens is often made in the first few years of marriage. The ignorance about the real demands of what it takes to make a marriage work makes some newly married couples conclude that perhaps the difficulties they're facing are unique to them. Some may even go as far as to conclude that they have married the wrong person. This obviously explains why most marriages that fail do so within the first ten years following the wedding ceremony. I've no hesitation in stating that marriage is a "garbage in, garbage out" type of undertaking. This means that what you put in is what you get out. You'll have a thriving marriage if you're fully dedicated to it. Similarly, if you're careless in your marital relationship, you'll have real problems.

The negative effect of our rapidly evolving world

Obviously, we're living in the digital age, where things move and change very fast. As a result, many expect that no human activity, including marriage, should be spared from that rapid evolution. Perhaps one needs to listen to some couples to understand the source of their perspectives about marriage. For instance, it's not uncommon to hear some people question why certain things should be expected of them in a marriage in this day and age. They don't necessarily question why certain things should be done, but rather why they should do them, given that we're now living in a post-modern world. Another example of a post-modern worldview is the effort a section of the society seem to be making toward the normalization of divorce. Many with such a view strongly suggest that the only remedy for a struggling marriage is divorce.

Lack of patience to learn about marriage

As it has been rightly called, marriage is an institution. Therefore, there's a lot to learn about it as an institution. And when you are a greenhorn, you need a lot of patience to truly learn and gain mastery of something. Before getting married, many people assume that they have a deep understanding of marriage and what it takes to lead a successful marriage. In fact, some were even bold enough to counsel others in their earlier days as unmarried people. It's probably true that some of these people had good theoretical knowledge of marriage. Unfortunately, once they get married and start facing the typical challenges most couples face, it comes to them as a rude shock, and only then do they realize that they know very little about marriage.

These issues, and many more, have been the inspiration behind this book. In the following pages, the reader will find important content and tools that, if applied with a sense of purpose, will reposition them to build a high-functioning marriage that they can be proud of now and in the years to come.

Key assumptions

I heartily welcome readers from all socio-cultural backgrounds and educational and religious persuasions. I pray that the book will be a blessing to every reader's life and strengthen their marriages. I assume that the reader understands the premise of this book, which is written primarily to strengthen family life, and the marriage institution specifically. It does not include life outside of marriage. It is not a one-size-fits-all manual. This book focuses only on what people need to know as well as do about marital relationships in a traditional family setting.

For that reason, it will be taking things out of context for men or women to seek to apply the provisions of this book or expect anyone outside of their marital relationships to treat them based on the provisions of this book. Additionally, as you read through these pages, the reader will see that I've been careful in acknowledging women's intellectual and leadership abilities, which they have been able to compellingly demonstrate in virtually all fields of human endeavor.

The third assumption is based on a question I've been asked by many on several occasions. That question is about what a spouse should do if their spouse sexually molests his own child. While I easily take for granted that imperfection is the weakness of us humans, I assume that certain despicable behaviors will not be associated with anyone's family life. This question is a good example of such despicable behaviors. My consistent response is that should such situations arise, you'll be perfectly in order to seek the advice of law enforcement agencies who are professionally and legally empowered to advise you on the next steps.

Finally, let me reiterate that this book will bless any reader who reads it. However, the spur I've received is to write a book that will be most beneficial to the following four main categories of people:

- **The happily married**
  You're leading a strong and healthy family life but are still looking for additional tools to make your marriage even stronger. You come from the perspective that there is always room for improvement in any human endeavor.

- **Those in an unhappy marriage**
  You're concerned that you're struggling in your marriage at this time, and you're actively looking for tools to help you turn it around and watch it flourish. This book provides important tools that are just right for you.

- **Those at the verge of separation or divorce**
  You're on the verge of giving up on your marriage, and you're asking yourself if that'll be the right thing to do. This book is for you because your questions have been sufficiently addressed.

- **Marriage counsellors**
  You're involved with marriage counseling either as a pastor or a lay person. This book would be an excellent addition to your existing toolkit.

"American society, through its institutions, must teach core principles: that marriage is the best environment in which to raise healthy, happy children who can achieve their potential and that the Family is the most important institution for social well-being. To set about the task of rebuilding a culture of Family based on marriage and providing it with all the protections and supports necessary to make intact marriages commonplace, federal, state, and local officials must have the will to act.[10]"

- Patrick Fagan and Robert Rector

PART ONE

Subtle Marriage Lubricants

- Chapter One: The Power of Agreement
- Chapter Two: The Therapeutic Power of Apology
- Chapter Three: Let your Spouse be Enough
- Chapter Four: The Power of a Wise Counsel

"Not many married people know that we exist. Even those who do hardly take us seriously as they should. However, those who are thoughtful and wise enough to take us seriously often rejoice that they did."

– Anonymous

CHAPTER ONE

THE POWER OF AGREEMENT

In Amos 3:3, the Bible tells us that two people cannot walk together except they are in agreement. This biblical provision is something anyone who has ever been in any type of relationship probably knows well. Any human relationship that is bereft of agreement will not be healthy. Such relationships rarely last long because each party isn't working towards the same goal. Also, incessant disagreements often breed tension, which will, in turn, hurt the relationship. It is obvious that marital relationships, with their uniqueness, require a much higher level of agreement between the couple than any other human relationship there is.

Agreement as a relationship-cementing concept is something that requires conscious effort from those involved. Verbal arguments are almost always present in marriages that are deficient in agreement. Sometimes those arguments degenerate into physical brawls. It is common to hear neighbors of households where domestic violence is prevalent come out to report routinely hearing loud verbal arguments from such households, typically after an incident involving bodily injury or even loss of life has occurred.

SUBTLE MARRIAGE LUBRICANTS

It is not unusual for couples to disagree. In fact, having a difference of opinion on issues comes from our ability to think, which is an essential part of being human. However, it is vital that if couples must disagree, they should try and put a positive spin on it. Couples should be watchful to ensure that disagreements between them are not increasing in frequency, as that will not be a very good situation. I believe that disagreement between couples should be driven solely by their mutual desire to arrive at a better outcome, rather than to massage their egos with a sense of "I am good, and you are a jerk."

Maturity in marriage

The need to entrench and dwell in harmony is one more reason to justify the point that marriage is ideally meant for mature adults. By maturity, I don't necessarily mean physical age. Rather, I mean one should possess the capacity to reason and behave maturely. Maturity also includes the ability to make thoughtful decisions and choices.

For example, a mature adult knows how to avoid discussions that will result in or tend toward unnecessary arguments. If a conversation veers towards an unhealthy end, a mature and sensitive adult will recognize it and change the subject. Even when a discussion ends up in an argument, mature people know how to steer it in such a way that the relationship is left unscathed.

Mature adults are also keenly aware that it is hardly helpful to always insist on having their way at all costs in a healthy relationship. It also takes maturity to disagree while carefully listening to others' points of view. Only a mature adult knows that it is unhealthy to insist on your point of view even if it means losing the other party. In marriage, mature adults know that to have your way at the expense of your relationship is a very unwise thing to do.

Unfortunately, couples with some gaps in their maturity development seem to feel a sense of gratification once they win an argument. Marriages that are fraught with arguments stand the risk of falling apart at some point unless the couple comes to their senses and takes steps to change their behavior.

As I relate to couples, it has been my observation that many people who have relationship management problems are usually quick to concede that no marriage is perfect. Such people often seem unwilling to exercise any self-control or make the required effort to ensure peace in their marriage. To help such people, I somewhat agree with them that it is probably true that many marriages they know of are imperfect, but I also try to make them realize that theirs doesn't have to be one of them! I usually charge such couples instead of setting a very low bar for themselves to strive toward perfection and stop hastily concluding that marriage, by its very nature, cannot be perfect.

> *... it is probably true that many marriages they know of are imperfect, but I also try to make them realize that theirs doesn't have to be one of them!*

Several years ago, I accepted a new role at a major upstream oil and gas company in downtown Calgary, Alberta. Within a couple of weeks, I met a colleague, and we started getting to know each other. This was when the US and its allies were fighting the twin wars in Afghanistan and Iraq.

My friend's views about the wars were utterly different from mine. His bias regarding the situation was simply too apparent and difficult to ignore. As a result, I also had to take my position firmly. The topic of the wars came up fairly frequently during our informal meetings. And on each occasion, we both stuck to our usual views.

One day, during such discussions, my friend asked me a question that I took to heart regarding arguments and interpersonal relationships. Because of how strongly we both felt about our views, he asked me this question: "Do you know that if we fail to agree on one thing, the chances are good that we will disagree on many other things in the future?"

I don't think my friend was suggesting that we should always agree on everything. That will not be a realistic expectation. In a way, he was unconsciously paraphrasing Amos 3:3. It is important for people to be in agreement in order for them to work together harmoniously over the long term. This is especially true for people who are in a marital relationship.

> It is important for people to be in agreement in order for them to work together harmoniously, over the long term.

The benefits of working in agreement

It is impossible for me to over-emphasize the importance of working in agreement in a marital relationship. Our Lord Jesus taught those who were listening to him on a certain occasion that a house that is divided against itself is guaranteed to fall. (Matthew 12:22-28)

SUBTLE MARRIAGE LUBRICANTS

Let us also learn an important lesson from the biblical account of the Tower of Babel in Genesis 11. We learn from that scripture that the whole world had a common vocabulary and used the same words at one time.

In the course of time, they began to say to one another, "Let's make bricks and thoroughly bake them with fire and let's build a great city for ourselves with a tower that reaches into the sky. This will make us famous and keep us from being scattered all over the world" (Genesis 11:3).

As they began executing this grandiose project, the Lord came down and saw the city and the tower the people were building. The Lord said, "Indeed the people are *one* and *they all have one language*, and this is what they begin to do; now nothing that they propose to do will be withheld from them. Come, let Us go down and there confuse their language, that they may not understand one another's speech" (Genesis 11:6-7).

The key phrase in this scripture that binds these people together is "one language." These people actually had a common human language with which they were communicating. Because there was no barrier to communicating what they wanted to do, the Lord knew that it would be easy for them to work together and complete their project. God saw the power that was available to these people – one language.

> "Come, let us go down and there confuse their language, that they may not understand one another's speech" (Genesis 11:7).

We can call this "one language" agreement in our day and by way of practical application. They were saying the same thing, they believed the same thing, and they were inspired to execute a historic project as a united group of people. They weren't working at cross purposes. They set their minds to work toward a common goal. They were united in spirit and in purpose.

Then, God determined that because the power of agreement was at the heart of what these people were doing, he knew it was impossible to stop them from accomplishing their goal. Obviously, God has unlimited ways that he can use to frustrate man's plans. However, in this particular situation, God identified the power of a common language available to these people to frustrate the construction of the Tower of Babel. Consequently, he confused their language and caused them to stop understanding one another.

And truly, the moment their language was confused, and they could no longer understand one another, they became thoroughly frustrated and were left with no other choice but to go their separate ways. The construction of the Tower of Babel was abandoned simply because of one thing: the language barrier or multiplicity of languages among the people.

Therefore, a couple that finds it easy to come to an agreement on issues in their marriage can be described as having one language between them. That is, when a couple is saying the same thing, understanding one another, setting goals, and communicating effectively among themselves, it will be much easier for them to set and achieve goals as a couple. And ultimately, their marriage will thrive and be blissful.

SUBTLE MARRIAGE LUBRICANTS

In one of his teachings in Matthew chapter eighteen, Jesus said, "If two of you agree on earth about anything they ask, it will be done for them by my Father in heaven" [Matthew 18:19 New King James Version (NKJV)]. That's what a couple that works in agreement stands to gain in their marriage – they often receive answers to their prayers.

> *A couple that always finds common ground on all issues enjoys a happy, fulfilled, tranquil, and long-lasting marriage.*

In the same vein, a couple that finds it difficult to reach an agreement on issues can be likened to a group of people who are supposed to be working together but unfortunately, between them lies a language barrier. They are constantly working against each other. Sometimes, there is a subtle spirit of unhealthy competition among them. When that becomes the case, they'll see themselves seemingly working so hard but struggling to achieve any meaningful results.

As in the experience of the Tower of Babel, persistent disagreement or lack of unity of purpose between a married couple is a risk to the sustainability of any marriage. But get them to communicate and understand, and work in agreement, and a sweet and blissful marriage will result. A couple that always finds common ground on issues enjoys a happy, fulfilled, tranquil, high-functioning, and long-lasting marriage. And they are also able to achieve tremendous success, even in terms of material and wealth accumulation.

SUBTLE MARRIAGE LUBRICANTS

Adolf and Eden's story

For example, a few months ago, I got a call from a young man from North-Western region of Florida named Adolf. He spoke with a shaky and beaten-down voice, asking, "When can I call you back so we can talk?"

As he sounded flustered and desperate, I enquired why he wanted to talk to me. He said,

"Pastor, I have lost my family."

I asked him, "How? Tell me, what happened? Did they get burnt in a house fire?"

He continued, "I beat my wife, and she called the police on me. Right now, as we speak, I have been given a restraining order which bars me from going close to my family."

After hearing his side of the story, I also called his wife, who provided a more vivid account of what transpired.

According to his wife, Eden, "My husband and I were playing Ping Pong outside with our eleven-year-old son. After some time, I left to go and do some chores. About an hour later, I heard my son scream out so loud, so I quickly ran outside to find out what had happened to him.

"The boy explained what happened." Eden continued. After hearing from my son why his dad beat him up, I reminded my husband about the law prohibiting parents from spanking their children."

SUBTLE MARRIAGE LUBRICANTS

According to Eden, "I firmly told my husband not to beat the boy ever again because I don't want to be guilty by association. If this boy reports the matter to his teacher at school, Children's Services will get involved, and it will become a major legal problem, including taking the children away from us."

On hearing these words, Adolf erupted and turned his rage on his wife. He said, "Let me tell you, Eden, you have no right to tell me how to parent my son. You know quite well that this boy is very stubborn, as he always insists on having his way. Therefore, if I don't discipline him now that he is still young, his stubbornness will get out of hand."

The exchange continued from there, and things completely went out of control. As a result, Adolf gave Eden the beating of her life and even threatened to use a kitchen knife to stab her to death if she dared challenge him again. Eden, being afraid for her life, called the police.

This was a classic case of a combination of immature behavior and a lack of self-control. Without any doubt, Adolf is the father of their son, but he fails to realize that he couldn't deny Eden the honor of being their son's mom. Therefore, with a little bit of reflection and self-control, Adolf would have acknowledged his wife's essential role in raising their children, and the situation wouldn't have degenerated into what it came to be.

Liam and Doofan's story

Another fascinating example of a senseless disagreement involves Liam and Doofan. This Fraser Valley, British Columbia couple had a needless disagreement that put them in an embarrassing situation. This is how Doofan narrated the situation to me:

SUBTLE MARRIAGE LUBRICANTS

Liam is a technology enthusiast. He can't resist buying the latest piece of technology that comes on the market. In fact, he'd rather buy the latest gadget, even if it means going hungry with his family. Liam readily admits that he derives great joy from being among the first to own the latest gadgets.

As usual, when Apple released iPhone 11 Pro Max, Liam desperately wanted to buy it. Unfortunately, he did not have the money to make the purchase. On this fateful day, we were on our way back home from visiting a friend. Liam brought up the issue of wanting to buy the iPhone 11.

Liam said to his wife, "I really want to get the iPhone 11. Unfortunately, as you know, I don't have money at the moment. So, when we get home, could you kindly give me your credit card to order it online?"

According to Doofan, she was the primary income earner at the time. So, she reasoned and reminded her husband, "But must you buy it now? Perhaps, you should wait until you have money. Why the rush?" Liam confessed to Doofan, "You know my weakness with technology. I'd rather have it now that it is red hot before it becomes commonly available. Besides, you know me as someone who is usually at his best when I've got the latest piece of technology."

Doofan replied, "Even if you were to buy it with your money, I'd still suggest that the iPhone 11 should not be your priority considering the current state of our finances. But it's even worse that you're asking me to give you my credit card. I am sorry, but that is not going to happen. I will not allow you to put that expense on my credit card."

SUBTLE MARRIAGE LUBRICANTS

Doofan continued, "You're always in the habit of frivolous spending using credit cards, leaving me to service the debts. Don't forget that I'm still paying for the iPad and Bang & Olufsen google speaker you bought with my credit card last Christmas."

She concluded in frustration, "I am getting fed up with your propensity for debt accumulation. Please, Honey, grow up! After all, you already have an iPhone 10." I'm going to ask you to use what you have pending when you have money to buy the so-called latest gadget."

On hearing these words, Liam's ego was crushed, and he quickly became very angry. He then parked the car off a busy street (he was the one driving), came down, went to the passenger's side where Doofan was sitting, and opened the door while threatening her to give him her purse.

Doofan was still adamant and wouldn't release her purse. At this point, Liam decided to snatch the purse by force, and a scuffle ensued.

Liam and Doofan could have avoided this situation with a little commonsense and flexibility. When couples take such non-negotiable positions in the event of a disagreement, the outcome can be anything. Experience has shown that when such disagreements occur once, their chances of repeating become more common. When that happens, the marital relationship may end in an unfortunate state.

My recommendation is that all marital disagreements be respectful, with the consciousness that you should never lose your partner in the process. It shouldn't be difficult to see the foolishness that is embedded in an argument you have won but has bruised your relationship. Therefore, if a couple must disagree, do so wisely, maturely, and with self-control for the sake of your marriage.

> *Never rush through a decision. If it must be rushed, then don't even give a thought to it.*

Expressed differently, disagreements between couples should be tactful, respectful, and with the sole purpose of exchanging ideas to arrive at a decision that will be in the best interest of their marital relationship.

Disagreement between couples should come across in these suggested formats: "Sweetheart, did you think about this or that option at all?" Or, "Honey, I think it'll be better if we take this route because of so and so reason." Better still, another spouse may say, "Darling, perhaps, we should sleep over this to give us more time to think about it." When a contrary viewpoint is expressed so tactfully and respectfully, it opens doors to more thought-provoking ideas and, ultimately, a healthier and more desirable outcome.

In our own way of ensuring that we are constantly working in agreement, if we have divergent viewpoints about a situation, my wife will say, "Honey, go ahead and decide, and I'll abide by your decision." On my own part, I respectfully make sure that I give her sufficient so that she's truly comfortable with the decision that I'm about to make before we finalize and move on to implementation.

SUBTLE MARRIAGE LUBRICANTS

> *When a contrary viewpoint is expressed in such a tactful and respectful way, it leads to more thought-provoking ideas and, ultimately, a healthy outcome.*

I don't ram through any decisions. I make sure that I'm completely thoughtful about every decision I have to make. In fact, my philosophy for making decisions that impact my family goes like this: "Never rush through a decision. If it must be rushed, then don't even give a thought to it."

If you have to wait for a year for your spouse to be on board with a decision, for the sake of your relationship, please, do it. The health of your marriage is worth the wait. If you've got to, I'll counsel that it is sound wisdom to abandon any decision that your spouse is not able to be on board with.

Some keys to achieving agreement in marriage

A high-functioning and blissful marriage is very possible. And anyone who desires a blissful marriage and takes the necessary steps towards actualizing it can experience it. As I've said more than once in this book, I find that one of the important keys to eliminating squabbles or disharmony in marriage is to whole-heartedly recognizing who has the decision-making responsibility in the home.

Tommy and Jayla's story

Statutorily, in God's unquestionably flawless wisdom, the decision-making responsibility rests with the husband. This responsibility has nothing to do with who is more intelligent or earns more money. I once knew a couple, Tommy and Jayla, who were classmates during their undergrad days. During their school days, Jayla used to score higher marks than Tommy, who is now her husband. Simply put, Jayla used to be a "straight A" student.

After they got married, Jayla would criticize almost every decision that Tommy made. In fact, more often than not, she would not only criticize Tommy's decision-making ability, but Jayla would go as far as reminding Tommy during disagreements not to forget their school days. She would say, "Look, Tommy, intelligence doesn't diminish. Once intelligent, always intelligent. I am still that same brilliant girl that you used to know during our school days." On one of such occasions, she invited Tommy to stop thinking he was smart simply because they were now husband and wife.

How many would argue that no married person should have that kind of arrogant thought process? The wife must show that she recognizes and supports her husband's decision-making responsibility. Husbands appreciate this recognition. But beyond his appreciation, the greatest benefit of this recognition is that God seems to back the husband in his decisions. When God backs the husband to make wise decisions that lead to good outcomes, the family – the wife and her children – are the direct beneficiaries.

However, the husband must be careful not to be found guilty of unilaterally making decisions in the home. The husband must endeavor to consult and leverage his wife's wisdom and commonsense that women are reputed for possessing. A husband who makes decisions without first seeking his wife's input is doing himself and his family a serious disservice. I

SUBTLE MARRIAGE LUBRICANTS

strongly recommend that all major or minor decisions be made with the wife's input.

> *A husband who makes decisions without first seeking his wife's input is doing himself and his family a serious disservice.*

The husband must demonstrate humility as he discharges his responsibility as the maker and owner of decisions in the home. Discharging this responsibility with humility makes you a servant leader. And as it were, leaders with a servant's heart usually reap the benefit of having an unalloyed following from the led. Family dynamics are no different.

Like every other young and inexperienced person, I made decisions that seemed trivial at the time but turned out to have far-reaching ramifications. I, therefore, determined in my heart that once I got married, my wife would always be my confidant and adviser. That's how I've come to rely so much on my wife for virtually every decision that I've had to make. And I have to admit that my wife's ability to help me connect the hidden dots is priceless.

KEY TAKE AWAY

- Agreement between a husband and his wife is necessary for them to build a blissful, long-term marriage.

- In marriage, mature people typically exhibit the following interpersonal characteristics. They:
    - Are skillful in managing conversations that have a potential to end poorly.
    - Are skillful in steering conversations in such a way that leaves the relationship unscathed.
    - Hardly insist on having their way at the expense of their relationship.
    - Know that in a relationship, it is unhealthy to have their way at all costs.

- A couple that finds it easy to come to an agreement in their marriage can be described as having "one language" between them.

- It is foolish to argue and lose or damage a relationship.

- In the event of an argument, argue wisely, maturely and with self-control for the sake of your marriage.

- It is wise to abandon any decision for which your spouse is unable to be on board with.

- A husband must demonstrate humility as he discharges his responsibility as the decision-maker in the home.

- A husband who makes decisions without first seeking his wife's input is doing himself and his family a serious disservice.

CHAPTER TWO

THE THERAPEUTIC POWER OF APOLOGY

An apology is a regretful acknowledgment of an offense or failure. Typically, this comes when someone accepts that they have done something wrong or has exhibited a behavior that falls short of what is expected of them. For an apology to have the desired effect, it must be accompanied by a sense of remorse. An apology from a spouse should be accompanied by a confession that, indeed, what they've done is disappointing and certainly does not reach the expected standard of conduct.

In James chapter five, we have this charge: "Confess your sins to one another, and pray for one another, so that God can heal you. When a believing person prays, great things take place" (James 5:16). Clearly, the healing referred to by James is the healing of sickness and diseases. But let me suggest that nothing hinders us from extending it to also include the healing of relationships. And beyond any doubt, genuine confession and apology have been shown to heal relationships.

When people in relationships are hurt, they become emotionally and psychologically sick. Those sickness can sometimes fester and spread to other parts of their physical bodies. As a result, when the guilty party repents and admits their shortcomings, all areas of the relationship that were harmed have a better chance of healing.

The Bible tells us something profound in the book of Corinthians regarding godly sorrow. That passage says, "Now I rejoice, not that you were made sorry, but that your sorrow led to repentance. For you were made sorry in a godly manner, that you might suffer loss from us in nothing. For godly sorrow produces repentance leading to salvation, not to be regretted;..." (2 Corinthians 7:9-10).

Most people know that the path to attaining a high-functioning marriage with near-zero disagreement is typically preceded by an initial period of occasional rough patches. Experience has shown that the closer you are to someone, the greater the likelihood of offense occurring, at least occasionally.

When an offense occurs in a relationship, confession and repentance are usually required to restore healing and trust. Andrew Guerra reiterates social psychologists' findings that a genuine confession, apology, and repentance have the potential to lead to forgiveness; it can repair a damaged relationship and may also heal indignity. Furthermore, he said that sincerely saying, "I am sorry," means that you have chosen your relationship over your ego. This sounds very beneficial and simple, yet so many of us strangely can't find the strength within ourselves to admit our fault.

> *Saying, "I am sorry" implies choosing your relationship over your ego.*

The benefits of apologizing

The short phrase, "I am sorry," appears quite simple, but it is very important since it has the potential to smoothen out any conflict and re-establish a deep connection with the other partner. This phrase is short, but when used with a genuine heart of repentance, its soothing impact on a strained relationship can be phenomenal. If you are sincere with your apology and repentance, it will go a long way in helping you eliminate relationship stress. It will also give you the strength to move on from conflicts and tensions to a healthier and more fulfilling relationship.

The following are some of the proven benefits of apologizing:

- The phrase "I am sorry" offers two benefits: first, it restores the dignity of the hurt person; and second, it makes them feel better—which is healing both at the emotional and psychological levels. The offended party, who receives the apology, develops empathy towards the offender, transforming their feelings of hurt into forgiveness.
- A genuine repentance can restore trust and understanding between parties in a relationship. It contributes to a feeling of safety and makes both the receiver and the giver feel comfortable and respected. Therefore, repentance following an offense helps you and your spouse stay emotionally connected and strengthen the bond between the two of you.
- As Guy Winch, psychologist and author of Emotional First Aid[14], reckons, *"An effective apology doesn't just heal the wound for the other person, it'll dissolve your guilt too."* Eventually, you will develop a sense

of self-respect and the ability to move on quickly. Normally, it also serves as a deterrent, so that you don't repeat the same mistake again.

Tips for making a genuine confession, apology, and repentance

The following tips will guide you if you truly want to confess and repent of a wrong-doing and make the offended spouse feel better:

- *When you are sorry, mean it for what you have done.* A former president of South Africa, F.W. de Klerk, once said: *"Deep regret goes further than just saying you are sorry. Deep regret says that if I could turn the clock back, and if I could do anything about it, I would have liked to have avoided it."* But before apologizing, recognize and acknowledge your fault and make the apology specific. For example, you can say something like this:, "I am sorry I ignored the conversation with you last night." It will show that you really understand what you did wrong. So, always speak from the heart and make the apology sincere. Words that come straight from the depths of the heart are usually obvious and hard to ignore.
- *Take responsibility for your actions.* You should never try to be defensive and don't look for excuses and explanations. The message, *"I take responsibility for being angry and hurting you during our discussion earlier today. I didn't mean to. And I am sorry,"* is direct, strong and effective. Avoid any "buts" in your speech, as including them in your apology means you're justifying why you offended in the first place,

which will not help your case very much. In fact, your apology will be rendered less effective when you try to justify why you did what you did. It also means that you actually did it on purpose.

These two clues will help show that you really do want to heal the hurt you have caused and rebuild trust in your relationship with your spouse.

Let me be clear: an apology will never make up for the offense that was committed. An offence can't be taken back or nullified once it's been committed. However, an apology can help relieve tension, the stress, and pain caused by the offense. Confession, apology, and repentance provide hope for rebuilding a bruised relationship. If you value the relationship, then a sincere apology and repentance can reposition the relationship on a path of trust and health.

Why is it that some people find it difficult to say, "I am sorry?"

With all its critical therapeutic benefits, many of us still find it so hard to verbalize this simple short phrase, "I am sorry." Obviously, there are several reasons why that's the case. According to Andrew Guerra, the most common reasons include the following:

- Many people erroneously believe that you admit that you are wrong when you apologize, which directly threatens our egos and our pride. You should learn how to be objective, and admit your mistakes, and not allow your egocentrism to blur your vision. However, if an apology wrecks your ego and pride, then perhaps, make sure you avoid doing anything that will offend your spouse in the first place.

- Confession and apologies are viewed as means to draw attention to the mistake or offence that has occurred. As a result, this often leads to a misguided implication that it's better to ignore or pretend that offense has not occurred, and hope that no one will notice. Such insensitivity is unhelpful and is not recommended. Remember our Lord's teaching:

"Therefore if you bring your gift to the altar, and there remember that your brother has something against you, leave your gift there before the altar, and go your way. First be reconciled to your brother, and then come and offer your gift" (Matthew 5:23-24).

In addition, Paul said, "… do not let the sun go down on your wrath, nor give place to the devil" (Ephesians 4:26-27).

Time is always of the essence when seeking to resolve a misunderstanding and restore peace with your spouse. Leaving it to fester is giving place to the devil. It is important to note that he will be glad to go multiple folds when you give the devil one chance.

- The person thinks that he or she is the one who deserves an apology first, so they wait for the partner to apologize. But this can be toxic for the relationship. Don't wait. Take the first step; apologizing will only increase your self-respect, not diminish it.

SUBTLE MARRIAGE LUBRICANTS

- Some people assume that confession and apologies are signs of weakness, but actually, they are hallmarks of strength. In fact, mature, emotionally healthy, and astute individuals find it easier to say "I am sorry" for what they might have done wrong. It is an act of generosity and an expression of hope for a struggling relationship. It is also an act of bravery because it subjects people to the risk of humiliation.

KEY TAKE AWAY

- Repentance implies that you are sorry for what you have done, and you have turned away from it.

- Confession, apology, and true repentance together have proven therapeutically effective in healing and resetting bruised relationships.

- A genuine apology implies that you've chosen your relationship over your ego.

- A genuine confession, apology and repentance have the power to rebuild damaged trust and ultimately reset a relationship.

- Genuine apology must exclude justifications for why the offence was committed, as such justifications risk nullifying the expected effect of the apology.

CHAPTER THREE

LET YOUR SPOUSE BE ENOUGH

We've all probably heard of the commonly used saying that "the grass is always greener on the other side." Unfortunately, it often appears to be greener from afar only because the observer often fails to look at it up close. Many people have reported being gravely disappointed after carelessly treating or even throwing away what they had, thinking that what was out there was much better. In any case, even if the grass happens to be greener on the other side, a spousal relationship is uniquely too important to be thrown away in anticipation that another spouse will be a much better person.

I'll have to repeat this fact that—the best time to decide if your spouse will be "good enough" for you is during the courtship period. If approached intentionally, the courtship period gives you the best opportunity to make that important decision. That is the best time to decide if you are happy and proud of your partner's personality, height, weight, chosen profession, level of intellect, and what he or she does for a living.

I have had to deal with ridiculous cases of spouses complaining about their husbands' low intelligence quotient, height, and earnings, many years into their marriage. Once you decide that he or she is the ideal person for you, it is best to stop looking for somebody more handsome, beautiful, intelligent, petite, richer, and taller than your spouse.

> *Unfortunately, it appears to be greener from afar only because the observer often fails to look at it up close.*

The cost of your spouse not being enough

You need to learn very early in your marital relationship why it is necessary for you to leave no doubt in the mind of your spouse that you are completely satisfied with him or her. If you fail to clearly show that satisfaction to your spouse, you may be risking losing your spouse. This doesn't necessarily mean separation or divorce. Sometimes, couples may be living in the same house, but their relationship is anything but a true marriage. To some extent, such a couple has lost each other while still living in the same house. When that happens, it'll ultimately be the fallout of his or her ill-advised behavior that may be rooted in discontent.

It's also important to note that losing your spouse is unlikely to happen all at once. It is usually a gradual and long process. One of the first critical steps in that process could be that the ungrateful spouse starts looking outside to try and get what they believe they deserve but is lacking in their marriage. This is precisely how covetousness starts, manifesting in different ways, including infidelity.

We learn from 1 John 2:15-17, which says: "Do not love the world or anything in the world. If anyone loves the world, love for the Father is not in him. For everything in the world—the

SUBTLE MARRIAGE LUBRICANTS

lust of the flesh, the lust of the eyes, and the pride of life—comes not from the Father but from the world. The world and its desires pass away, but whoever does the will of God lives forever." The lust of the flesh, the lust of the eyes, and the pride of life can show up in several ways, such as an unreasonable quest for material possessions, social status, etc.

It's usually not too difficult for the spouse who is not seen as enough to realize it. The wavering commitment of the offending spouse to the marriage can quite easily become evident. When his or her commitment is questioned, the marriage becomes unstable, which is usually difficult to pretend about.

> *It is usually not too difficult for the spouse who is not seen to be enough to realize it.*

Grant and Aver's story

A few years ago, a beautiful couple, Grant and Aver, were having some challenges in their marriage. When they brought their situation to my attention, and we started discussing it, at some point during the discussion, Grant asked his wife, "Can you also help me understand, in the presence of Pastor Mannie, why you keep making fun of my height?"

When I demanded to know what that meant, Aver did not mince words at all. She confessed that to be completely honest, it was her life's longing right from her teenage years to marry a six-footer and not the short man Grant is. It was an evening of full disclosure, and Grant decided I needed to know about one striking incident that occurred.

SUBTLE MARRIAGE LUBRICANTS

And he began, "It was a beautiful spring evening two years ago. Aver and I went shopping at Chinook Mall. With her obsession with tall men, Aver saw a tall, nice-looking guy who passed us and was going in the opposite direction. She couldn't resist and repeatedly turned to look at the guy. Little did she realize that I was observing what she was doing. Unfortunately, she missed her step in the process as the floor level in the expansive mall changed. As a result, she tripped and fell. I lovingly helped her up."

Grant continued, "When we finished shopping and were driving home, I again told her how sorry I felt to see her trip and fall, but I told her that I felt it was important to let her know that I knew what happened and also how disappointed I was with her. So I asked Aver, "What were you turning repeatedly to look at? Is it possible that you were looking at some guy?' Aver became furious and very defensive. Then she asked me if anything was wrong with me. She became angry that I was wrongly accusing her of looking at some guy. Then she momentarily bursts into tears and started sobbing."

On hearing this fresh narration of that embarrassing episode, Aver couldn't look up anymore. At that point, I gently helped her to understand how important it was for Grant to know that he's the ultimate person in her world. To further lighten the mood in the room, I jokingly told her, "It isn't possible that you are just realizing that your husband is not a tall man. Neither had Grant suddenly shrunk in height since you got married to him."

SUBTLE MARRIAGE LUBRICANTS

Jim and Danica's story

Danica and Jim were lovely middle age couple. One day, they went to pay a visit to their family friend who had just moved into their brand new in-fill home in the Upper Mount Royal neighborhood, an upscale community adjacent to Calgary's Central Business District. Danica and her friend, Inga, were high school classmates. Out of nowhere, Danica and Jim started having needless arguments following that visit.

According to Jim, Danica started harassing him by insisting that they must also buy a house in Upper Mount Royal. Jim tried all he could to let his wife understand that, given their present financial situation, it would be foolhardy for them to go out and buy a home in that expensive neighborhood. Jim added that he repeatedly told Danica that they simply couldn't afford a home in that community at the moment.

Jim continued, "One particular night, Danica woke me up in the middle of the night and asked me, "Jim, can I ask you a question?" I agreed to answer Danica's question. "Can you tell me if Inga's husband has two heads that he is able to buy a house for his family in Upper Mount Royal, and you keep saying you can't?" Jim confessed that this question hit him so hard. However, "I managed to control myself by taking a long pause while thinking about the best way to answer my wife."

Jim continued with his narration, "Danica obviously didn't like my long pause at all. In fact, it would seem as if she was determined to get on my nerves that particular night." So, she decided to repeat the question, "Are you not the one I am talking to, Jim? Or are you becoming hard of hearing?" Jim tactfully asked his wife, "Please, can we talk about this tomorrow?" "No!

SUBTLE MARRIAGE LUBRICANTS

Let's talk about it now. Sorry, but I need the answer now, or we will both stay awake until daybreak." Danica insisted.

According to Jim, after another long pause, he cleared his throat and started, "Well, you know how upset I feel when you keep comparing me with other people. The other day, it was Mike, our neighbor, who bought a Porsche. More than once, you have compared me with your brother-in-law, who takes your sister on so-called exotic vacations; today, it is Inga's husband. You seem to imply by your incessant comparisons that I've never done anything for you that is worth remembering since we got married. But that's okay."

"Anyway, to answer your question, let me say that, obviously, Inga's husband doesn't have two heads. However, as you probably are aware, it is still possible that even people with only one head can sometimes be different."

"Thank God," Jim continued, "I am not Inga's husband. I am Danica's husband. That alone is the most important difference between him and me. Does that answer your question or not?"

Danica reminded Jim, "Don't forget the old saying, 'Happy wife, happy life.' If you want to know, I am not a happy wife at all. Let's see how you will have peace in this house." Then she said good night, turned and gave Jim her back, and then slept off.

Over the weeks and months that followed, things began to boil out of control, and I got involved. After listening to this couple, I reminded Danica about 1 Timothy 6:6, which says that godliness with contentment is great gain. I assured her that Island Estates at Mahogany, where they were living, was equally an upscale and highly desirable neighborhood. I further told her that it was still possible for them to live in Upper Mount Royal one day if that was her ultimate desire. But she should note that there is the right timing for everything. With prayers and a bit more talking, God took control of the situation.

Dear reader, comparing your spouse with another person is a grave mistake and very disrespectful. Such a comparison can be very demoralizing to anyone, to put it mildly. The only message such a comparison conveys is that your spouse is not good enough, and the person you are comparing him or her with is much better. Furthermore, it shows that you do not appreciate your spouse as a special gift that God has given you.

> Above all, it shows that you do not appreciate your spouse as God's special gift to you.

How to demonstrate complete satisfaction with your spouse

There are simple yet powerful and effective ways to show your spouse that he or she is all you have. Therefore, instead of comparing your spouse with other people, you need to always be on the lookout for opportunities to praise him or her and to highlight how special they are.

Rather than making him or her look incapable, you should never forget that you are the best person to make him feel capable, significant, and even indispensable. Let your spouse know that he or she is simply the best. Let your spouse know, and be sincere about it, that, as far as you are concerned, there is no human being in the whole world who is better than him

SUBTLE MARRIAGE LUBRICANTS

or her. Tell him or her when they least expect just how grateful you are to God for giving him or her to you as a lifetime gift.

Personally, I am always at ease at every opportunity that I have to assure my wife that if I were to choose who to marry all over again, she would still be my first pick. What about you? When last did you assure your spouse that you never made a mistake in marrying him or her? When last did you assure him or her how blessed you feel about having him in your life as a spouse? Such assurance will go a long way toward strengthening your marriage.

> *Personally, I am very much at ease at every opportunity that I have to assure my wife that if I were to choose who to marry all over again, she would still be my first pick.*

KEY TAKE AWAY

- The ideal time to decide if your spouse will be good enough for you or not is during courtship, not after you have gotten married. Once you wed him or her, settle down and whole-heartedly appreciate your spouse every day of your life.

- A spousal relationship is too precious to carelessly abandon in the anticipation that another person out there will be a better spouse.

- Lack of contentment with your spouse exposes you to the risk of covetousness, which can lead to some moral failures, including adultery.

- Use these practical ways to demonstrate your contentment with your spouse:

    o Be sensitive to opportunities to acknowledge and praise your spouse for his or her unique personality and strengths.

    o Let your spouse know that there's no human being out there that is better than he or she is.

    o Let your spouse know how grateful you are to have him or her as a gift from God.

- Husbands, let your wife know that choosing her as your wife is the most thoughtful choice you have ever made. Assure her that if given another opportunity to choose, she will still be your first choice.

CHAPTER FOUR

THE POWER OF A WISE COUNSEL

"Where there is no counsel, the people fall; But in the multitude of counsellors, there is safety" (Proverbs 11:14).

If you've read through Chapter Five of Volume I of this Family Life Handbook series, you would've noticed that I took time to emphasize the need to carefully listen to what trusted adults, who have your well-being at heart, may have to say about your dating relationship. I believe it is a sign of wisdom to intentionally look for and establish a relationship with some people in your life that you trust and can readily go to when you need direction in your marriage. On the other hand, I'll say there is very little wisdom for someone to arrogate to themselves all knowledge and wisdom while ignoring or even despising good counsel that may be available to them.

Let me stress that, in general, the courtship and the marriage phases are quite different. When you leverage such wise counsel during your courtship period that leads to marriage, you're not yet done with leveraging wise counsel. Therefore, I'll suggest that the nature of the counsel you'll need during these two phases will also be different.

SUBTLE MARRIAGE LUBRICANTS

As the passage above says, you're at great risk of failing when you do not have people you can turn to for counsel. Similarly, those who surround themselves with wise counselors are in a very safe position. Experience has shown that when you're in the midst of a situation, you can easily miss some important viewpoints, no matter how long you stay in that situation. But the moment you bring in an external person with fresh eyes who is neutral towards the situation, he or she will likely see all those perspectives you never saw. That's the benefit of having a good counselor or advisor. With those fresh eyes looking into the situation, a wise counselor can guide you into seeing other perspectives that could help resolve the impasse in your marital relationship.

Often, marriage provides pleasant experiences. However, sometimes some experiences may not be very pleasant, especially in the early days of many marriages. It's important not to read too much meaning into everything. Try and take things easy, as there may be no cause for alarm after all. If you handle those not-so-pleasant experiences carefully, you may discover that the situations were only there as good opportunities for you to learn and grow as a married person. In other words, you turn those situations around for your good and the good of your marriage. However, if it's something that lingers on and even begins to give you cause for concern, then don't hesitate to seek counsel on time.

I've heard about some couples who staunchly refused to seek counsel even when their marriage was in real trouble. One of our pastor friends told us about an experience he had with a couple in their church. This couple was struggling in their marriage so badly. So, the wife decided to mention it to my friend. After considering the matter, our friend and his wife

SUBTLE MARRIAGE LUBRICANTS

decided to go and visit them so they might provide some help. But before visiting, my friend told this woman's husband why they would like to visit them.

> *If you handle those not-so-pleasing experiences carefully, you may discover that the situations were only there as a good opportunity for you to learn and grow as a married person.*

My friend and his wife got to this couple's house on the agreed date. As they settled down and began to discuss the issues, the husband became agitated and started wondering why their pastor found it necessary to come and talk to them about their marriage, which he reasoned was a personal and private matter. In fact, my friend confessed that it was one of the most awkward situations in which they had ever found themselves. As a result, they could not make much impact on the situation as the husband stonewalled them. Unfortunately, the marriage fell apart not long after that meeting. It's quite possible that if this woman's husband had been open to getting the help they clearly needed, the outcome would probably have been different.

Beyond any doubt, your marriage is indeed a "personal and private affair." However, the reality is that sometimes you'll need to step out of that "personal and private affair" mindset and get the help you need to save your marriage and even reposition it to thrive. And in many such situations, time is often of the essence.

I strongly believe there's no shame in asking for help when needed. Of course, you may end up living in denial for some time so that no one knows you are struggling in your marriage.

SUBTLE MARRIAGE LUBRICANTS

But, as the saying goes: You can deceive others, but you cannot deceive yourself. Sure, no one may know that you need help, but will that be the reality? Unfortunately, when you fail to get the help you need, and your marriage fails, all you might have been keeping personal and private will become known to everyone around you. One wonders what's the wisdom in that kind of attitude.

When should you seek counsel?

If you are not able to resolve your differences, it's advisable that you consider seeking counsel sooner rather than later. I have heard some people naively suggest that you should leave the situation for some time, and it'll probably resolve itself. It is not likely that a marital conflict will just resolve itself simply because you have left it alone long enough. In fact, it may actually get worse and even affect other aspects of your relationship. That's why it is important to seek counsel as soon as possible so you can resolve your disagreement and get back to enjoying your marriage.

Who should be your marriage counsellor?

The initial and most important counsel should come from God. And that is usually through prayer and your knowledge of God's Word. You'll need to take the time to pray about the situation as a couple and ask God for his intervention. But the important caveat here is that you should be able to hear the voice of God and discern the direction he may be providing in the situation. It is critical to take the time to prayerfully discuss it with an open mind. If you both know yourselves well enough, you may be able to discuss and resolve the disagreement. And that will be great.

SUBTLE MARRIAGE LUBRICANTS

It bears repeating that it takes some wisdom to carefully look for some adults that you can trust and whom you can go to for counsel when you need it. And I say with a high degree of probability that you will likely need counsel at some point in your marriage. For most Christian couples, the natural choice of a counselor could be their pastor, although it doesn't have to be. I say this because I know that not all pastors are in a position of strength to confidently assist others who may need help with their marriage.

Usually, your parents, though capable, may not be in the best position to be effective marriage counselors for their own children. Parents may be tempted to take sides, thus blurring their sense of objectivity as humans. But if they are your pastors, then, of course, they may be able to help you.

Therefore, I recommend that you look for a couple whose family life you admire and whom you can look up to. Such a couple doesn't have to be pastors. But it is important that they are Christians. Try and make this identification early on in your relationship. That gives you enough time to get to know the couple well so you can feel comfortable going to them when you need help.

I love books, especially good Christian books. I'm sure you do too. And it certainly is not a bad thing to be an avid reader. To that end, some good books will help to enrich your marriage. Look for such books and read them together as a couple, ideally when things are still normal in your marriage.

I highly recommend reading good quality books because of the power of being knowledgeable in all the important areas of one's life. Obviously, the Bible says that "My people are destroyed for lack of knowledge…" (Hosea 4:6). Many couples struggling in their marriage are doing so simply because they lack the requisite knowledge necessary to sustain a healthy and long-lasting marriage. And many more don't have sufficient knowledge about their specific marital responsibilities. And a great source of that knowledge is reading and receiving solid counsel when required.

> *And it certainly is not a bad thing to be an avid reader.*

As you read good books on marriage to inspire you to lead a healthy and high-functioning marriage, you'll also get to know some authors and counselors through their writings. Some of such counselors may be within reach when you need them, but others, not so much. If you've developed confidence in them through their writings, their books may be an important reference material for you, especially in times of need.

Your choice of a counselor should be predicated on the trust you've reposed in them. That way, you can vouch that what they will tell you will be Spirit-led and biblically-based. Let me suggest that it would not be particularly safe for you to simply go online and query Google for a marriage counselor in your area without knowing their pedigree. The risk of doing so is that you may end up with more misguided counsel than you ever imagined. Therefore, you would want to do some homework before deciding who to go to for counsel.

KEY TAKE AWAY

- He who seeks wise counsel is in a safe place.

- He who despise wise counsel risks failure.

- First and foremost, it is important to learn to take your marital challenges to God in prayer and trust him to help you resolve the challenge.

- Identify couples you admire whose family life you can look up to as your counselor.

- Seek counsel on time for a situation that may be causing stress in your marriage.

- It is not very helpful to leave a disturbing situation on its own with the hope that it will resolve itself with time.

- Ignorance can be destructive to a lot of things, including marriage.

- Actively seek knowledge about marriage as an important part of your overall development.

- If it is possible, avoid going to a marriage counselor that is not a Christian or whose pedigree you are unsure of.

PART TWO

Marital Responsibilities for Husbands

- Chapter Five: The husband's unconditional love for his Wife
- Chapter Six: Nourish, Cherish and Care for your Wife
- Chapter Seven: The husband's leadership role to his Wife

"Husbands, love your wives, just as Christ also loved the church and gave Himself for her,... So husbands ought to love their own wives as their own bodies; he who loves his wife loves himself."

[Ephesians 5:25, 28]

CHAPTER FIVE

THE HUSBAND'S UNCONDITIONAL LOVE FOR HIS WIFE

The husband must completely and unconditionally love his wife. That is the biblical standard God has designed for his children to follow. Complete love simply means there is absolutely no reservation in how a husband loves his wife. It also entails loving her to the point of accepting death and allowing his wife to live if necessary! Anything less than that is incompatible with Christ's self-sacrificial love for us. When he offered himself for us, our Lord Jesus loved us unreservedly, and the price he paid for our redemption symbolizes complete and perfect love.

Unconditional love implies accepting your wife for who she is. Indeed, as Paul has stated in the verses above, the husband does himself a favor when he unconditionally loves his wife. She doesn't need to do anything special to win her husband's affection, and she doesn't need to be perfect to be the love of her husband's life. After all, you are not flawless either. The fact that she is your wife is the sole reason you should love her unconditionally. That's it. She has earned your affection by accepting your proposal to be your wife. Unconditional love for your wife is a sign of obeying a scriptural injunction. When

MARITAL RESPONSIBILITIES FOR HUSBANDS

a husband loves his wife, he follows the example established by Christ himself.

> It also means loving her to the point that if it becomes necessary, you can accept to die and let your wife live!

The fifth chapter of Romans teaches us something so profound. It says that for we know how dearly God loves us, and we feel this warm love everywhere within us because God has given us the Holy Spirit to fill our hearts with his love. When we were completely helpless, with no way of escape, Christ came at just the right time and died for us sinners. Even if we were good, we really wouldn't expect anyone to die for us, though, of course, that might be barely possible. But God showed his great love for us by sending Christ to die for us while we were still sinners. Romans 5:5-8

These verses accurately reflect our situation: we were given what we did not deserve or earn. Similarly, I'm sure your wife would cherish your unconditional love for her, especially since you didn't make her do anything special or act in a certain manner to earn it.

The inherent need of a woman

Certainly, there's a very good reason why God commands husbands to love their wives. And regardless of their cultural or socio-economic background, I believe women have an inherent need for love. It won't be an exaggeration to say that every woman craves love. She was conceived and born with that craving, and it isn't something that she developed over time.

MARITAL RESPONSIBILITIES FOR HUSBANDS

That is, without a doubt, why God commands husbands to love their wives.

As a result, it is not surprising to realize that love is one of the most important things that makes a woman secure in a marriage. I know many women well. However, I have not met one who seeks a divorce because her husband loves her too much. Very recently, one of our friends confirmed this same thing. She said, "All a woman needs is to be sure of her husband's love. Once she secures that assurance, the husband can guarantee her total commitment to the marriage."

> It is safe to say that every woman craves love.

I've seen a nine-year-old girl express this desire just like a woman at ninety-nine does. Quite naturally, for an adult female, the most appropriate person to satisfy that need is a man—ideally, her husband. That way, she is certain that the love is not transient but that it's guaranteed to always be there for her.

Not very long ago, a family friend, who had worked in one of the Middle Eastern countries with a notoriety for repressing women, told us a touching story about the plight of women in that country. Typically, as their culture allows, a man will marry several wives and keep them all in one big and nice house. If he can afford it, he will sometimes keep his wives in separate locations across the city. The husband will lavish them with jewelry, clothing, shoes, and whatever else money can buy. He will keep them in high-walled houses where they are customarily not allowed to step outside. If they do, it must be with a male's approval. Sometimes, such a male may be the woman's son. Sadly, the mother will have to get permission from

The Husband's unconditional love for his Wife

MARITAL RESPONSIBILITIES FOR HUSBANDS

her son to go outside the home. The wives will dress up, put on expensive jewelry pieces, and stay indoors every day. They call it "dressing to the delight of the husband."

Outwardly, these married women appear to have everything going for them. Unfortunately, the deprivation and limits they are exposed to are usually too tough on them to put into words. Many of these women confided in our friend, one after the other, about how miserable they were. According to them, they had pretty much everything that could be purchased with money. However, all they were starving to death for was love. Some even said they felt like household furniture, as their husbands showed no love at all. Most of the women wanted to find out if our friend could arrange men from her home country who would be willing to marry them so they could taste what love from a husband really was.

This narrative is an example of just how the heart cry of every woman is to experience genuine love from her husband. This desire is real regardless of the woman's ethnic, educational, or religious background. This also shows that God has genetically configured us with the ability to feel and experience love. When it is lacking in a relationship, we know it as humans. This is especially true for the female gender.

The second reason it is essential to love your wife is that you do yourself a huge favor by doing so. Loving your wife conveys the impression that you also love yourself. It also shows that you understand one of the most basic rudiments of marriage. That very basic understanding says that the husband leaves his father and mother and be joined to his wife, and the two shall become one flesh.

MARITAL RESPONSIBILITIES FOR HUSBANDS

Here are a few ways the husband can demonstrate his love to his wife:

Verbalize your love to your wife

I once heard a woman describe it this way: if you love me, say it, and then show me. Both the saying and the showing of love are necessary and pleasant for the well-being of your wife. Like some of those Middle Eastern men described above, they thought they were showing love to their wives by buying all the expensive things out there to be bought with money. But as their wives loudly stated, that was not nearly enough because those material things were given with no affection or thoughtfulness whatsoever. To put it another way, your wife expects to see you in whatever gift you give her. Otherwise, your gift will not be well-received and, as a result, will have minimal impact on her and, ultimately, on your marital relationship.

When used together thoughtfully, these three words, "I love you," form one of the most powerful sentences that can stir up positive emotions in the person receiving them. The more your wife hears them, the more the words positively impact her. Women say that men use the words "I love you" very generously in the early stages of a long-term relationship, and this is probably true. However, when time passes and they marry, they rarely use those words to their wives.

For that reason, some women may go away with the impression that men say "I love you" only to get their wives hooked. But if the husband doesn't want her to hold such an impression of him, he'll need to continue letting his wife know that he genuinely loves her long after the wedding day. So, men, "I love you" are magical words that should be used in your marital relationship

MARITAL RESPONSIBILITIES FOR HUSBANDS

for the rest of your life. Your wife will never tell you, but she will always expect you to tell her.

In some cultures, it is an alien idea for husbands to verbalize their love for their wives. It is not necessarily forbidden; but you hardly hear men say it to their wives. Unfortunately, in such cultures, that pattern runs from one generation to another. Other men carelessly say something like this: "But my wife already knows that I love her without a shred of doubt. What is the point of saying it repeatedly?" Such men usually ask with little thought or emotion.

Not very long ago, I heard a widowed Canadian music icon openly admit on national TV that what she misses most is hearing her husband tell her that she is beautiful and that she is loved. These words, "I love you," are so amazingly powerful and reassuring. They are excellent for your wife's emotional and psychological well-being and also great for keeping your marriage healthy. You have them, so be generous with them.

> These words, "I love you," are amazingly powerful and reassuring. They are excellent for your wife's emotional and psychological health.

Further in his Ephesian epistle, Paul rightly wrote that no one ever hates his own flesh but nourishes and cherishes it (Ephesians 5:29). Therefore, loving your wife as a very important part of your own body is just the natural thing to do. The reverse—that is, not loving yourself—is unnatural. Husbands, be natural and love your wife unconditionally and completely.

MARITAL RESPONSIBILITIES FOR HUSBANDS

Therefore, if you haven't told her that you love her today, put this book down, walk over to her, and tell her these exact three words. If she is not close by, pick up the phone, call or text her, and tell her that you really love her. Don't put it off for another time. Do it now.

> *If she is not close by, pick up your phone, call or text her, and tell her that you really love her.*

Let her see you in the gifts that you give her

A gift that's given with deep thought often leaves a deep impression on the receiver. That kind of gift-giving leaves a long-lasting positive impression on your wife. For that reason, no husband should give his wife a gift solely for the sake of gift-giving. Do your best make ensure your wife can easily see your heart in the gift.

Love by being sensitive to your wife

The Bible says this: "Husbands, likewise, *dwell with them with understanding, giving honor to the wife*, as to the weaker vessel, and as being *heirs together of the grace of life*, that your *prayers may not be hindered*" (1 Peter 3:7).

This passage contains very important counsel that we must all take the time to understand and take to heart. To emphasize and help us understand this passage better, I have italicized some key phrases that make this passage very important.

The first part of the passage enjoins husbands to **dwell with their wives with understanding.** We can paraphrase these words like this: "Husband, you must make every effort to live with your wife based on your knowledge or understanding of who she is. Your wife is a unique individual with a unique personality and character. That's why the husband must spare no effort in making sure that he understands his wife well."

This knowledge includes everything about your wife, ranging from her family background, strengths, weaknesses, temperament, likes, and dislikes. Knowing her family background is crucial since our upbringing has a significant impact on the core and essence of our being. Intellectual, social, organizational, and work habits, among other things, will be among the strengths and weaknesses. Knowing her strengths and weaknesses will give you the basis for setting realistic expectations of her.

Temperament is vital because it will help reposition you to manage her emotions. Know what to say or do and know *when* and *how* to say or do it. Make no mistake, the importance of knowing your wife cannot be overstated.

Considering Peter's counsel, I would advise husbands to view marriage as an institution where they have enrolled to study and manage their wives' personalities to glorify God together in your marriage. And that study will last a lifetime. Expect unannounced quizzes, tests, and examinations along the way in your learning experience, just like you would in many other institutions of study. Husbands should be aware that they will be graded informally, with a passing or failing grade.

If you know your spouse well enough, you'll always get high scores no matter how many times you're tested. And how well you do will reflect on the health of your marriage. To have a healthy marriage, you must first know your wife well and then

MARITAL RESPONSIBILITIES FOR HUSBANDS

use that knowledge to relate to her. You will be a good student if you let this principle guide you.

Ron and Tammy's story

A few years ago, a couple close to my wife and me, Ron and Tammy, found themselves in an unnecessary conflict that escalated into a physical brawl while driving home from a weekend getaway. Once they managed to get home safely, Tammy drove straight to our home to report her husband. My wife and I decided to follow her to their house after hearing her side of the story so we could hear from Ron.

After hearing from both sides, I indicated to Ron that, as the husband, he should have handled the situation differently to avoid the embarrassment of publicly fighting in front of commuters on the side of a busy street. Ron was infuriated when he heard this. "Pastor, you are saying this because of your ignorance about who this woman really is," he interjected.

He said this with a raised voice and a pointed finger at his wife. He then added, "All you have known so far about this woman is her soft side. I bet you, when you will eventually see her hard side, then you will know who she really is."

I politely asked Ron to stop right there. I told him that I could be pardoned for my ignorance about his wife's personality because she is not wife. I suggested that with what had just happened between them, he too was ignorant of who his wife really was. This was my counsel for him: "Had you known her well, you would have leveraged that knowledge to manage your relationship with her better. A discerning and astute husband knows how to de-escalate marital conflicts by taking his wife's personality and character into account."

> *A discerning and astute husband knows how to de-escalate marital conflicts by taking his wife's personality into account.*

Honor your wife

Honoring your wife simply means displaying or exercising a high degree of respect or esteem for her. As I meet with people from various backgrounds, I've seen that few people have the grace or courteous goodwill required to esteem others.

My observation is that people frequently appear to believe that by not honouring others, they are elevating themselves. Some people, sadly, carry that undesirable behavior into their marriage. When I hear a husband command his wife to do something in front of visitors, it makes me unhappy. My typical response is to reduce the number of times I visit such homes. I don't feel at ease being a guest in a household where the wife is dishonored and treated like a domestic servant.

Perhaps, the wife may not feel humiliated or dishonored, most probably because she is already accustomed to her husband's demeaning behavior. In some cases, her cheeks may just drop in shame. But such husbands must remember to ask themselves, "Where is the biblical honor my wife is entitled to?" Honor dignifies, while dishonor demeans.

When you treat people with honor and dignity, you cause the best to come out of them. The opposite is also true; you hurt

MARITAL RESPONSIBILITIES FOR HUSBANDS

their spirit, drive, and self-worth when you demean, shame, or humiliate someone. Is that what you want to see in your wife? Do you want to see your wife living like a defeated bully victim in her own home?

> But the husband must ask himself, where is the biblical honor that your wife is entitled to? Honor dignifies, while dishonor demeans.

The last part of that verse says something that should make every husband much more careful in managing their marital relationships. It says: ... **so that your prayers will not be hindered.** This statement means knowingly or unknowingly doing something whose resultant effect leads to the subversion of your prayers.

Any Christian who does something to obstruct their prayer is unwise and an enemy of themselves. That's precisely what a husband faces when he doesn't put in the required effort to study and thoroughly understand his wife, when he doesn't honor her and fails to regard her as a joint heir of the grace of life.

Husbands, the benefits, or lack thereof, of honoring your wife have been placed back in your laps. There is a lot in it for you when you honor your wife. Why would you want to subvert your prayers? Why will you be laboring so hard with very little to show for it? Why will you live your life as if you were swimming upstream against the tide? Why will you be sabotaging yourself? These questions are some of the illustrations of what it means to live in the realm of hindered prayers.

MARITAL RESPONSIBILITIES FOR HUSBANDS

Don't be like some husbands I have known who go after their wives as being responsible for their sub-optimal success in life. Leave her alone—she is not personally accountable for your average life. In fact, she may even be praying very hard and wishing you well. However, the way you manage your relationship with her may have brought all kinds of chaos into everything you do.

I'm not implying that a life of mediocrity is only related to how you manage your marital relationship. Not at all! Various additional physical and spiritual factors could be at play. However, when the result of your efforts is inconsistent with what is expected of a married man, Apostle Peter advises a husband to ensure that his relationship with his wife is not a contributing factor in his search for the reason(s).

I have heard some Bible commentators try to explain the phrase "…so that your prayers may not be hindered…" to simply mean loss of ability to concentrate during prayer only at a particular time. Somehow, I find such an explanation to be an oversimplification. However, even this oversimplified meaning should still be unacceptable to any discerning husband.

As a Christian, I believe anything that affects or inhibits your prayers, whether briefly or over time, must be dealt with forcefully. This is because, as most spiritually awake people are aware, one of the first targets of the enemy is the believer's prayer life. As a result, you won't want to allow anything to get in the way of your prayers. You must take steps to nip it in the bud!

KEY TAKE AWAY

- The husband should love his wife completely and unconditionally.

- Loving your wife is meeting one of her most important yearnings.

- The husband that loves his wife unconditionally is demonstrating that he loves himself.

- A gift that makes an impact on your wife is a gift that's given with careful thought behind it.

- Some examples of how to show your wife that you love her include:

    - Verbalize your love for her as frequently as you can.

    - Let her see you in the gifts that you give her.

    - Be sensitive in your dealings with her.

- Make every effort to know your wife's personality as much as possible.

CHAPTER SIX

NOURISH, CHERISH, AND CARE FOR YOUR WIFE

So husbands ought to love their own wives as their own bodies; he who loves his wife loves himself. For no one ever hated his own flesh, but nourishes and cherishes it, just as the Lord does the church. Ephesians 5:28-29

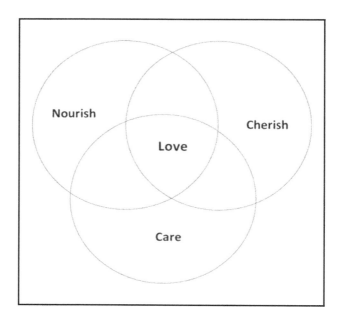

Figure I: Love: Nourish, Cherish and Care Interconnection

MARITAL RESPONSIBILITIES FOR HUSBANDS

The Venn diagram above helps explain the interconnectedness of the four words: nourish, cherish, and care, and how they are all bound together with love at the center. The diagram shows that if you cherish your wife, you will take very good care of her. And if you *nourish* her, you are doing so because you *cherish* and deeply *care* about her. Ultimately, all three are motivated by the love that you have for her.

In the book of Ephesians, Paul aptly suggests that no one ever hates their bodies. Rather, everyone knows how to take time to nourish and cherish their body. He made this analogy to draw husbands' attention to their wives. For that reason, husbands must learn to nourish, cherish, and care for their wives. The word "nourish" simply means *to provide with food or other substances necessary for growth, health, and good condition*.[11]

It should be evident to anyone that nourishing means providing food to someone. But the above definition adds a significant dimension to the meaning of the word nourish. Let us take a closer look at the second part of that definition which includes "...*other substances necessary for growth, health, and good condition.*" Growing and being in good health or condition entails much more than physical growth. One may physically grow as tall and as big as possible, but such growth doesn't necessarily always indicate healthy growth. Neither does it mean that such a person is in good condition.

The definition above more accurately talks about *health* and *wellness* to express it more succinctly in today's everyday language. Again, we need to properly understand what "*health* and *wellness*" means. These two terms are commonly used to

MARITAL RESPONSIBILITIES FOR HUSBANDS

describe what it means to be in a balanced and healthy state of well-being.

According to the Substance Abuse and Mental Health Services Administration (SAMHSA) organization, "wellness" is often used interchangeably to denote good health or to rate a person's overall health[12]. However, wellness has much broader implications. While health generally refers only to a person's physical and sometimes psychological health, wellness assessment takes several factors that can affect one's health into account. Such factors include *stable relationships, exercise, nutrition, access to clean water, and the safety and security* of a person's living situation. These factors often predict long-term wellness because, even if a particular issue currently does not affect a person's wellness, it can, eventually.

SAMSHA has identified eight dimensions of wellness to focus on to optimize one's wellness. The eight dimensions include: emotional, spiritual, intellectual, physical, environmental, financial, occupational, and social. Lack of support, trauma, unhealthy thinking styles, chronic illness or disability, and substance abuse can also compromise wellness.

As a caring and loving husband, you can see how indispensable it is for you to ensure that your wife is in optimal health and wellness by providing her with proper nutrition. This obviously extends well beyond ensuring that her pantry is stocked with food and that her fridge and freezer are filled with all perishable foods. We now know that you must strive to satisfy your wife's emotional, spiritual, environmental, intellectual, and social needs in addition to providing nutritious nourishment.

MARITAL RESPONSIBILITIES FOR HUSBANDS

Emotional

Having your wife's emotional needs met start with **sharing and caring for her**. A wife who feels loved, cared for, and appreciated is far more likely to be emotionally healthy. They are more inclined to reciprocate if she knows her husband cares for her and will always be there for her through big and small events, resulting in a healthy marriage.

Spiritual

Make every effort to pray and study the Bible with your wife regularly. In my experience, I believe this is the simplest and most effective way to lead your wife. You'll also need to actually engage your family in a local church. You can also get good books to read and discuss together. Furthermore, you can find conferences that enrich your lives spiritually to attend together regularly. Find teachings, messages, and other spiritual programs on TV or online to watch together.

Environmental

The environment in which we live can facilitate or discourage interactions among people. In fact, the environment can influence people's behavior and motivation to act in a particular way. For example, a comfortable home with privacy can go a long way in making a wife feel secure and cared for.

Intellectual

On the other hand, the intellectual dimension entails connecting beyond just the physical and emotional levels. When two people in a stable and healthy love environment stimulate and enrich

MARITAL RESPONSIBILITIES FOR HUSBANDS

each other's minds, the relationship has a strong potential for intellectual intimacy. Couples with a higher percentage of intellectual connection are often happy since minds with comparable intellectual values can bond more firmly.

Here are some ways to build intellectual intimacy in relationships.

Cultivate shared interests

Cultivating a relationship where you and your partner share intellectual interests become highly beneficial. Having similar perspectives on the world and similar viewpoints on news, debates, and other topics helps form a strong bond and, most importantly, a significant amount of mutual support.

Read together

Books are the most effective way to enrich one's mind and expand their vocabulary. And, to be honest, they aren't many better ways to bond than by reading good books together. Having a weekly book club is an excellent way to connect more intellectually. Therefore, you and your partner should choose books jointly to read.

Share views

When it comes to political beliefs and opinions, many couples tend to have disagreements. However, if you and your partner endeavor to share the same values and notions about honesty, justice, rights, etc., intimacy builds. Experts believe that when partners share similar beliefs, they are more attracted to each other.

MARITAL RESPONSIBILITIES FOR HUSBANDS

Social

Women need affection in a myriad of ways. You may cringe at the term "public displays of affection," or PDA, but the truth is your wife just needs you to hold her hand. We don't want to make out in front of strangers any more than you do, but an arm around your wife's shoulders or a gentle and loving touch shows that she is the #1 person in your life. Demonstrating deep affection for her convinces her that you're proud to be her husband.

Needless to say, women like to talk, and that's no secret to anyone. Talking is a basic way for them to express themselves. When you tune out as a husband, your wife feels like you don't care. So, if your wife says she wants to talk, turn off the TV, put down your phone, and open your ears.

Cherish your Wife

Let's look at the term "cherish" now that we've understood the meaning of the word "nourish" in a marital setting and how it influences marriage success.

The husband must also cherish his wife. The verb "cherish" means to care for someone or something deeply, to treasure it, like how you cherish the time you spend with a favorite or special person you don't see often. That is how we treat our bodies because they are precious to us. That's how God expects you to cherish your wife. We must care deeply for them and treasure them because they are our gems.

MARITAL RESPONSIBILITIES FOR HUSBANDS

The criticality of communication.

Communication is the process of connecting and sharing yourself verbally and non-verbally so that your wife understands. She doesn't necessarily have to agree with everything you are saying. Studies show that couples who enjoy *real communication* frequently and effectively have a more engaging relationship. And couples who achieve deep levels of communication enjoy the greatest level of satisfaction in their marriage. In fact, I would say that if communication is the lubricant that oils relationships, then, it is safe to say that it actually serves as an engine that actually drives a marriage.

> *If communication is the lubricant that oils relationships, then it is safe to say that it actually serves as an engine that drives a marriage.*

Effective and meaningful communication in an intimate spousal relationship is the type of communication that fosters long-term connection and intimacy. We can use God's model of communication with us, his church, as a reference to understand this essential concept in the context of marriage.

Throughout Scripture, we see at least three fundamental levels that God has continued to communicate with us his children. You and your spouse can evaluate your communication effectiveness by asking yourself if the three levels discussed below are operational in your day-to-day interaction or not.

Information Level Communication

God went to great lengths in Scripture to share volumes of important and interesting information with us. He tells us how

MARITAL RESPONSIBILITIES FOR HUSBANDS

the heavens and the earth were created. He includes countless biographies of men and women who worked closely with him as well as individuals who refused a relationship with him. His Word, the Bible, contains in painstaking detail how his Son was born, lived, died, and was raised again to perfect the redemption of mankind. The Bible also describes the early decades of church history.

As a result, effective communication in a marriage must encompass all kinds of information. You must, for example, address the specifics of your personal schedules, finances, and childcare on a regular basis. Your spouse also needs to be aware of your daily activities while you are away from home, as well as your work projects, interactions with others, surprises, and any other events or occurrences that happened while you were apart. You invite your wife into your universe by sharing this information with her which goes a long to encourage profound intimacy in your marriage.

Communicate Opinions and Beliefs

Our opinions and beliefs may not be perfect like God's, but they are just as important in building intimacy in a marriage. Your spouse needs to know what you think about what's going on in the community and in the world. It pays a lot to stay informed, especially about local, national, and global affairs, which are mostly accessible these days via our mobile devices. When you share your thoughts and values with your spouse, you invite them into your thoughts, encouraging intimacy.

Communicate Feelings and Desires

Throughout the Bible, we find how God reveals a wide range of emotions, as shown in these scriptures—

MARITAL RESPONSIBILITIES FOR HUSBANDS

Joy: "And suddenly a voice came from heaven, saying, 'This is My beloved Son, in whom I am well pleased'" (Matthew 3:17).

Anger: "So the anger of the Lord was kindled against Moses, and He said: 'Is not Aaron the Levite your brother? I know that he can speak well. And look, he is also coming out to meet you. When he sees you, he will be glad in his heart'" (Exodus 4:14).

Jealousy: "For you shall worship no other god, for the Lord, whose name is Jealous, is a jealous God" (Exodus 34:14).

Love: "For God so loved the world that He gave His only begotten Son, that whoever believes in Him should not perish but have everlasting life" (*John 3:16*).

Grief: "And the Lord was sorry that He had made man on the earth, and He was grieved in His heart" (Genesis 6:6).

Disappointment: "I greatly regret that I have set up Saul as king, for he has turned back from following Me, and has not performed My commandments" (1 Samuel 15:11).

In very plain terms, the above examples tell us that God has emotions, and he reveals those emotions throughout his word. We also sense the yearnings of God's heart in his Word, his deep desire for a relationship with us, and his sorrow when we do not respond to his love.

Similarly, your spouse needs to hear not only your information and your convictions but also your feelings and desires about what is happening in your life. It means it's not wrong to describing what is going on in your heart with words such as, "I feel like…," "It hurts me when…," "I'm so happy about…," or, "I really wish that…." When you share your deep emotions and yearnings with your spouse, you welcome her into your heart, encouraging intimacy and trust.

Developing proficiency at all three levels is key for meaningful, intimacy-building communication. That is, being intentional about communicating to welcome your spouse into your world, your thoughts, and your heart. You must grow and become an expert at sharing what you know, think, and feel with your spouse. It will undoubtedly enrich your marriage.

> *That is, being intentional about communicating to welcome your spouse into your world, your thoughts, and your heart.*

Models of communication in marriage

Communication happens in three main ways: verbal communication, which refers to effective speaking; listening communication, which refers to active listening and, in turn, is the act of mindfully hearing and endeavoring to comprehend the meaning of the words being spoken by another in a conversation or speech; and non-verbal communication, on the other hand, refers to the tone and pitch of voice, including body language or gestures. Effective interpersonal communication must include these three areas.

One of the most critical areas of conflict in marriage is the absence of ongoing communication that gives your wife access to the core of your very being. I've found that many spousal conflicts can be traced back to a lack of this type of heart-to-heart communication between the couple.

MARITAL RESPONSIBILITIES FOR HUSBANDS

It's easy to see why communication between a married couple is even more valuable: they live together and sleep in the same bed night after night, so if they don't communicate effectively, there will inevitably be tension, which will eventually lead to conflict. I facilitate dialogues with couples during therapy sessions just to hear what they may have been holding within them which is typically an indication that they have not been actively and freely expressing their feelings or emotions to each other.

> *The absence of ongoing communication that gives your spouse access into your heart has been recognized as one of the important areas of conflict in marriage.*

Active listening is particularly important because it is the most effective approach to giving a communication feedback loop. According to communication experts, people often wait for the speaker to finish speaking before responding. Active listening entails paying close attention and making every effort to comprehend what is being said to give an appropriate and effective response. The resulting response may be poor, out-of-point, and even awkward if active listening is not used.

For example, it's natural for your wife to want to know how your day went and how your commute to work was, and she'll almost certainly ask you about the status of the project you're working on. She'll ask a few more follow-up questions based on your answers to these inquiries. Unfortunately, a typical husband may not always be in the mood to engage in such conversation right after getting home. He will probably prefer to relax, quietly reflect and unwind first.

MARITAL RESPONSIBILITIES FOR HUSBANDS

When the husband is not very responsive, his wife may not appreciate it at all. Of course, expecting the wife to "shut up" and stop "bothering" her husband is absurd. It'll be similar to getting a river to flow upstream. They want to talk to their husband, whom they haven't seen all day.

Therefore, the onus is on the husband to learn the act of patience and grow and develop good listening skills. He will also need to learn to respond to his wife to create an affectionate and engaging atmosphere in the home. For example, a husband may respond to his wife in this way: "I'm really tired tonight, but I'll definitely fill you in tomorrow." This way, communication is still being done while honesty and transparency are implemented. Such an atmosphere is important for the health of any marriage.

> *Unfortunately, a typical husband may not always be in the mood to engage in such conversations right after getting home. He will probably prefer to relax, quietly reflect and unwind first.*

KEY TAKE AWAY

It is important for husbands to carefully note the following:

- Real men habitually honor their wives because they know that their wives are God's special gift to them.

- You are responsible for creating a healthy marriage and home environment in which your whole family can thrive. Your children will thank you for it.

- Your wife will not become a better person simply because of your constant criticism and demeaning. In fact, she will become increasingly less of what you desire of her.

- You will see and experience the greatness of your wife when you love, pray, praise, and constantly highlight her strengths.

- The powerful combination of love, prayer, and praise have been tested and proven to inspire and turn weaknesses into strengths.

- Real men know how to nourish and cherish their wives so that their ingenuity can fully manifest.

- Real men love their wives to death.

CHAPTER SEVEN

PROVIDE LEADERSHIP TO YOUR WIFE

Paul wrote in his letter to the church at Ephesus in chapter five that wives should submit themselves to their own husbands in the same way that they submit to the Lord. He goes on to say that they should do this because the husband is the head of his own wife, just as Christ is also the head of the church. He concludes that, in the same vein, the church is subject to Christ. He enjoins wives to also be subject to their own husbands in everything (Ephesians 5:24).

It is common knowledge that leaders are responsible for providing direction and vision for the organizations they are leading. And just as leadership is crucial to the success of any organization, so it is to the family unit. In a family setting, the responsibility of leadership is given to the husband by God. The husband's leadership responsibility is in all areas, including but not limited to decision-making around spiritual matters and finances. As the leader, the husband also has the responsibility of setting the spiritual tone in his family. I'm delighted to say that in my interactions with couples from diverse cultural and socio-economic backgrounds, I've discovered that most women naturally look up to their husbands for leadership, which is beautiful.

However, there is a humorous aspect of this family leadership dynamic that is commonly joked about, especially in North America. In many parts of North America, husbands refer to their wives as the "boss." That is, when the husband makes a decision, he expects his wife to approve of it before it is implemented. Although that's a joke, I think that makes a lot of sense, as a leader is quite different from a boss. A boss more or less gives orders, while a leader takes the time to consider all options, including the potential consequences. That's why in this joke, the wife as the boss is waiting to either say 'yes' or 'no' to her husband's decision without necessarily being responsible for carefully considering all the options herself.

> A boss orders their direct report to do things, while a leader takes the time to consider all options, including the potential consequences.

In exercising his leadership responsibility, before the husband makes the final decision, the wife, who is a partner and deputy leader in the home, must always be consulted, and her opinion taken into account. The husband must be considerate and refrain from rushing into any decision, no matter how big or small.

Husbands should be aware that they will require the support of their wives during the implementation process. For the implementation phase to go smoothly, you'll need your wife to own the decision with you. Furthermore, it is a leadership best practice for the leader to consult the followers so feel that they are a part of the decision-making process. This also ensures that every facet of the situation is thoroughly explored. You

MARITAL RESPONSIBILITIES FOR HUSBANDS

never know when a fantastic idea will emerge from your team members as a leader.

Spiritually, the husband is the *pastor* of his household. That is part of what Paul meant when he said the husband is the head of his wife (Ephesians 5:23). Let me reiterate yet again that the husband's headship over his household is all-encompassing, including spiritual matters. As the popular saying goes, you cannot give what you don't have. Therefore, to be effective in his all-important leadership role, the husband should make every effort to grow and become spiritually grounded. At the very least, he must learn and know how to pray. He should also be a dedicated Bible student to provide good spiritual guidance to his family. He should study and be well-versed in teaching and leading his children as they grow up and guide his wife.

These days, there are many excellent Bible study classes or resources available online that people can take at their own pace and convenience. You might be able to find some part-time in-class Bible school opportunities depending on where you reside. The Apostle Paul counseled the young Timothy to study to show himself approved unto God; a workman that needs not be ashamed, but rightly dividing the word of truth (2 Timothy 2:15).

I strongly believe this important counsel is not just for pastors or other leaders who are in the pulpit ministry. Anyone who wants to grow spiritually can benefit from it, study, and become more grounded.

I have heard some people argue, "But we have a vibrant Sunday school at church that is tailored to children. Isn't that enough?" My answer to that line of argument is that a two hour Sunday

MARITAL RESPONSIBILITIES FOR HUSBANDS

school class once a week is not enough. However, I agree that it is a good starting point. Remember that you spend most of your time with your children at home throughout the week. Make use of some of that time to instill spiritual knowledge in them.

It is invaluable to show your family how important it is to actively live your Christian life daily. Therefore, the husband and father should endeavor to create a schedule for a daily family altar and be disciplined to follow it as faithfully as possible. To optimize this schedule, I'll emphasize the importance of self-discipline. Otherwise, competing priorities may take precedence over the time set aside for the family altar before you realize it.

> *Therefore, the husband and father should endeavor to create a schedule for a daily family altar and be disciplined to follow it as faithfully as possible.*

To make the family altar practical, effective, and productive, the husband and father should always make time and prepare ahead. A simple suggested outline to follow may look like this:

- **Take a few praise and worship songs.** Let this be a team effort. Encourage your wife and children to participate in the choosing of songs that you will all sing together. If singing is difficult for some family members, turn on some recorded music, sit back, and soak yourselves in it.

Personally, the reason why I love singing during worship as opposed to simply listening to recorded music is that I would rather use my voice and energy to worship than sit and listen to others worship my awesome God on my behalf. I have determined long ago that I will not hire others to worship God for me. I will gladly do it myself.

The most prevalent reason for people's aversion to singing during worship is that they don't have a good voice. When they listen to themselves sing, many report feeling ashamed. But I don't believe that's a good justification though. Such folks should be aware that God is only seeking true worshippers. He isn't seeking worshippers with a good voice.

- **Read from the Bible**. The husband and father would have prepared and identified a passage ahead of time. There are many good daily devotionals available these days. You can find some online, or your pastor may be able to assist you in obtaining one. You can also create your own Bible study plan.

- **Briefly explain the passage to your family**. Encourage your wife and children to ask questions about the passage or share what they've learned from it. I believe that teaching children to learn how to share from God's Word in a home setting is an excellent practice to adopt. The children gain confidence in communicating their understanding of the scriptures as they continue to do so. If they keep going, it will also help them improve their general communication abilities, an invaluable transferable skill that will come in handy in various situations in their lives.

- **Pray** – the husband must have prepared what to pray about ahead of time. To be organized, these prayer points could be written down. However, the family should be open to other prayer points that the Holy Spirit may be leading them to pray about on the fly.

I would recommend that every family member keeps a prayer journal where they write down their prayer points. A prayer journal will help you stay focused. It also holds a record of what you have been praying for. Furthermore, it brings a great sense of encouragement to see how faithful God is in answering our prayers. Our faith is strengthened when we see God answer our prayers, and we become more motivated and confident in our prayers as a result.

- **Closing prayer** – pray a prayer of blessing on the family. And bring the family devotion meeting to a close.

Again, the above outline is merely a suggestion. Every family should be able to follow whatever structure works best for them. The overarching goal here is to ensure that the family is consistently praying together and learning and growing in their knowledge of God and his Word.

People occasionally ask me how long a family altar should last, especially after I teach on the necessity of one. I don't recommend any length of time. It can last as little as twenty minutes or as long as everyone is still paying attention.

As children thrive better when given some routines, it will be great to set a time and stick to it. Anytime between dinner and bedtime would be a good time. Setting and sticking to a time for prayer also helps create a sense of keeping a scheduled appointment with God.

MARITAL RESPONSIBILITIES FOR HUSBANDS

The concept of a family altar aims to specify how to fulfill the famous passage of scripture which says a child should be trained in the way he should go so that when he is old, he will not depart from it (Proverbs 22:6). A child raised in this type of environment is more likely to understand the value of prayer in their personal lives and the family as a whole.

> *The concept of a family altar aims to specify how to fulfill the famous passage of scripture which says a child should be trained in the way he should go so that when he is old, he will not depart from it.*

According to studies, a considerable number of North American millennials from Christian families abandon their faith once they reach adulthood. Clearly, this is not good for the young people involved, their families, or the community as a whole. And ultimately, it is not good for the kingdom of God.

It is my modest opinion that to reverse this regrettable statistic, parents, especially fathers, should do much more to instill Christian values into their children very early on. I believe it to be a guaranteed safeguard against the ferocious bombardment that Gen Z and the Millennials will inevitably face as they grow up and leave home.

> *I believe it to be a guaranteed safeguard against the ferocious bombardment that Gen Z and the Millennials are inevitably going to face as they grow up and leave home.*

Some Christian parents suggest that children should be allowed to grow up and discover God independently, which is very disappointing. Unfortunately, I have yet to discover or hear the foundation of such an odd doctrine. I have every reason to doubt that such a position is based on God's Word. I am thoroughly bewildered at how a Christian parent will suggest that it is their children's responsibility to grow up and discover God themselves. Aren't we all living in a post-modern world where shopping carts labeled "Student Shopper" are specifically designed for young children? The concept is straightforward: teach children how to shop so that when they grow up, they will be ardent shoppers who will "shop till they drop dead!" How true and consistent is this with Jesus's saying that the children of this world are wiser than the children of light? (Luke 16:8).

> I am thoroughly bewildered at how a Christian parent will suggest that it is his children's responsibility to grow up and discover God themselves.

What about parents' deep involvement with their children's sporting activities? For many families that I know well, their involvement in taking their children around for sporting activities can rightly be described as temporarily putting their lives on hold while they support their children to develop sporting skills. Parents' effort in supporting their children to develop skills in playing musical instruments must also be highlighted.

What about being physically active, especially during the winter months, through outdoor activities such as skiing and skating? The involvement of parents in such activities is excellent and should be encouraged. However, I will add that parents will do well if they can add spiritual development to their must-do list to make sure the children are given the tools

MARITAL RESPONSIBILITIES FOR HUSBANDS

that will enable them to give spirituality the right level of priority as they grow up.

Paul has very apt instructions for parents and families today. In the fourth chapter of his first letter to Timothy, he stated how the Holy Spirit expressly tells us that in the last times, many will turn away from the true faith; they will follow deceptive spirits and misleading teachings that come from demons (1 Timothy 4:1).

According to him, these people are hypocrites and liars, and their consciences are dead. He told Timothy that if he explained these things to the church he was pastoring, he would be a worthy servant of Christ Jesus, one who is nourished by the message of faith and the good teaching he was a custodian of and has followed over the years.

He went further to admonish Timothy not to waste time arguing over ungodly ideas. Instead, he asked Timothy to train himself to be godly. He added this message that seems to clearly vary with a section of the church's value system today. He said that physical training is good, but training for godliness is much better, promising benefits in this life and the life to come (1 Timothy 4:8). He concludes that this is a trustworthy saying and that everyone should accept it. That's very true for us today.

The unfortunate thing is that parents are giving copious amount of their resources—time, energy, and money—to the physical training of their children. But they must ask themselves a crucial and necessary question: after the children develop their sporting skills and possibly make it to a professional sports league, earn a lot of money, and retire financially comfortable and secure, what next?

MARITAL RESPONSIBILITIES FOR HUSBANDS

That is the question on which we must all pause and reflect. The answers to these questions will assist us in developing a broad perspective on life. The right answer to that question, in my belief, is what King Solomon said in chapter one of Ecclesiastes. He said, "'Meaningless! Meaningless!' says the Teacher. 'Utterly meaningless! Everything is meaningless.' What do people gain from all their labors at which they toil under the sun?" (Ecclesiastes 1:2-3 NIV).

Of course, it is all the toil that we all go through in our very short sojourn on earth. Life is very short and even futile when viewed through the lens of eternity. And that's precisely the point Paul was making—training for godliness is profitable for all things since it holds promise for the present life and the life to come.

There's a lot more to life than pursuing this world's earthly pleasures. In addition, this world is far too short and temporary for us to devote our entire lives to it. True wisdom entails striking a healthy balance between these earthly pursuits and things that have eternal value.

KEY TAKE AWAY

- The husband is the leader of his household—that includes his wife and children.

- The husband, as the leader, sets the direction for his family—this direction includes spiritual, financial, moral, and so on.

- Most women look up to their husbands for leadership from a family perspective.

- The husband and father should develop a routine that would help raise his family in a godly way. Such routine should include a regular family altar.

- The husband and father should encourage his family to learn to share what they have understood from the word of God.

- A healthy and good balance between physical and spiritual activities is important for all of us, especially children.

- Our sojourn on earth is too short for us to devout our whole life to it at the expense of our spiritual development.

PART THREE

Marital Responsibilities of Wives

- Chapter Eight: Wife's Submission to Her Husband
- Chapter Five: Wife's Cheerleading Her Husband

"A wife of noble character who can find? She is worth far more than rubies. Her husband has full confidence in her and lacks nothing of value. She brings him good, not harm, all the days of her life"

(Proverbs 31:10-11)

CHAPTER EIGHT

WIFE'S SUBMISSION TO HER HUSBAND

Like the husband, the Bible has helped define the wife's responsibilities in a marital relationship. And as it were, God has hardwired the husband to desire his wife to discharge these responsibilities towards him. A Christian wife has two key marital responsibilities to discharge towards her husband.

These are:

- Submission
- Cheerleading

In the fifth chapter of his signature letter to the church at Ephesus, Paul penned these words: "Wives, submit to your own husbands, as to the Lord. For the husband is the head of the wife, as also Christ is head of the church; and He is the Savior of the body. Therefore, just as the church is subject to Christ, so let the wives be to their own husbands in everything." (Ephesians 5:22-24).

Just as the above passage explicitly links Christ's love for the church and husbands' love for their wives, he recommends that wives should ensure that their relationship with their husbands is as reverentially deep as their relationship with Christ himself.

MARITAL RESPONSIBILITIES OF WIVES

> Just as Paul explicitly linked Christ's love for the church and husbands' love for their wives, he recommends that wives should ensure that their relationship with their husbands is as reverentially deep as their relationship with Christ Himself.

Let me again implore every reader to think about the seriousness with which God treats marriage in the above three verses. I believe there is no better way for a Christian to emphasize the significance of a relationship than to compare it to our relationship with Christ. There can't possibly be a more stunning analogy than this.

Understanding what submission is not

As it pertains to Christian marriage, let's first start by eliminating what submission is not. But before we continue, let me appeal for an open mind so that the Holy Spirit may shine a new light into your spirit regarding this critical concept. I will recommend that everyone should approach this essential concept from the point of view that, most certainly, there is no biblical provision that seeks the subjugation of women.

> Before we continue, I appeal an open mind so that the Holy Spirit may shine a new light into your spirit regarding this important conceptual word.

It should also be understood that Christianity shows no tolerance for any form of demand for subservience. There is no second-class personality in Christianity—male or female. Before the sovereign Lord, we are all his first-class children.

MARITAL RESPONSIBILITIES OF WIVES

At the core of the Christian faith is freedom and liberty from every form of oppression, suppression, or subjugation. This fact is supported by what Jesus himself said in John's gospel in the eighth chapter: He said, if the Son of man makes anyone free, the person will truly be free (John 8:14).

Note the emphasis on the phrase *"truly free"*. This emphasis means that the freedom that is in Christ is unquestionably quintessential. It means freedom from repression, abuse, shame, authoritarianism, condemnation, poverty, sin, and ultimately from eternal damnation. There is absolutely nothing that is left out from the freedom that is in Christ Jesus.

Additionally, Paul specifically wrote in the third chapter of his letter to the Galatians. He said, "There is neither Jew nor Greek, there is neither slave nor free, there is neither male nor female; for you are all one in Christ Jesus" (Galatians 3:28). This passage simply says that in Christ, it doesn't matter if you are a man or a woman, a husband or a wife. You are important, and you should be treated as such. Expressed differently, the passage says that regardless of one's gender, ethnicity, or socio-economic background, we are all equally important in God's scheme of things. No one is superior to another.

> The freedom that is in Christ is unquestionably quintessential. It means freedom from repression, abuse, shame, authoritarianism, condemnation, poverty, sin, and ultimately from eternal damnation.

Now, submission is important to husbands at the same level as love is to wives. The word "submission" is becoming increasingly misinterpreted or misunderstood these days, and it will be best

MARITAL RESPONSIBILITIES OF WIVES

for many in some cycles if its use is avoided entirely. Some people would prefer that the word not be mentioned in any context where a marital relationship is being discussed. Thankfully, the biblical mandate for wives to submit to their husbands is for a good cause. As a result, it is important that we all pay attention to the word.

As I have said more than once, marriage is a spiritual undertaking, and as such, those who elect to participate in it should try as hard as they can to approach it through the spiritual lens.

> *Submission is important to husbands at the same level as love is to wives.*

Therefore, with the above preamble, let us try and rule out what submission is not. I believe this approach will assist in clearing up some of the misunderstandings that some people have, revealing the true meaning of the word "submission." I also believe that if people approach the Bible with an open mind, even the most skeptics will appreciate what it has to say about submission.

So, let's go. Submission in marriage does not include any of the following four scenarios described below:

The wife should not try to positively influence her husband.

Brett and Becca's story

There was a fine gentleman named Brett, who staunchly closed his mind to any teaching or discussion about tithing, out of stinginess. Brett refused to tithe, and he will ignorantly say he

MARITAL RESPONSIBILITIES OF WIVES

doesn't believe in the concept of tithing. He will oddly say, "I count myself among those who believe that tithing is a practice under the law, and it should not be a New Testament practice."

On the contrary, his wife, Becca, correctly understood the concept of tithing. In the meantime, the couple was operating a joint account. Becca will quickly calculate her tithe from the portion of their joint account and pay at her earliest opportunity during each pay period. And she did this very faithfully. This situation brought a severe conflict between Becca and her husband. He will tell his wife that it is his responsibility as the head of the family to approve how the family's money should be spent. Brett used every means in the book to discourage his wife from tithing.

Meanwhile, Becca stubbornly refused to cave into her husband's pressure. At some point, Brett started blackmailing his wife that she wasn't submissive to him. When the couple came up for a discussion with me, I discovered that their actual area of disagreement was on tithing, as Brett could not point out any other area of concern with Becca. Obviously, I congratulated Becca for standing for what is right. I also praised her effort toward being a positive influence on Brett.

The wife should forfeit her ability to think

Women are intellectually capable. As far as I am concerned, it is superfluous to say that no gender has a monopoly of superior intellect. The overall capabilities of some of these women have enabled them to climb high up the corporate ladder where they work. Therefore, it is unfair and even wrong to expect that they should hang up their strong abilities and cease to be intellectually engaging with their husbands once they come

MARITAL RESPONSIBILITIES OF WIVES

home. Being intellectually but respectfully engaging is not lack of submission at all.

When their brilliant wives present a superior case during conversations, some men become instantly intimidated. I think it's disingenuous for a husband to hide behind a complex and label that as lack of submission. Men should view their brilliant wives as assets, consider themselves fortunate, and begin utilizing their wives' competencies to establish a successful marriage.

The caveat I must add to this point is that brilliant and capable wives should avoid talking down to their husbands. They should endeavor to convey their ideas respectfully. Otherwise, their brilliant ideas will be useless if they lose their husbands by poorly and immaturely conveying them.

> *They must endeavor to convey their ideas respectfully. Otherwise, their brilliant ideas will be useless if they lose their husband by poorly and immaturely conveying them.*

The wife should maintain silence in the face of domestic violence or abuse

In many cultures around the world, domestic violence or abuse is frequent. In Canada and other regions of North America, it is likewise slowly increasing. It can sometimes be found even in Christian homes, which are supposed to be very peaceful. No one should condone domestic violence or abuse. Christian husbands are subject to the same laws necessary for society's peace and harmonious coexistence.

MARITAL RESPONSIBILITIES OF WIVES

Domestic abuse is strictly prohibited in North America and in most parts of the developed world. And all citizens, including Christians, are subject to the same laws. As a result, the wife is free to report any instances of domestic abuse perpetrated by her husband to law enforcement agencies. The wife who reports her violent or abusive husband to the police is not exhibiting a lack of submission.

As is well known, numerous incidences of domestic violence have resulted in serious bodily or psychological trauma or even death. As a result, every proven occurrence of domestic violence should be reported to the police to be handled appropriately to serve as a deterrent to the abuser.

> *If a Christian chooses to take the law into his own hands because of his physical strength that gives him an undue advantage over his wife, the law is there to protect the wife.*

No man should strive to earn the infamous title of being a wife abuser. That is a shameful title to hold. No one should find it difficult to realize how disgraceful it is for you to raise your hand to beat your wife. By beating your wife, you have effectively reduced her to a level below a human being.

Therefore, before you raise your hand against your wife, here is something you must remember: your wife is your most important partner in life, your soulmate, your teammate, your prime root, and most importantly, she is the same flesh with you. Think about that for a moment. The Bible says that you and she are one flesh. That's who she is, and you must treat her as such.

MARITAL RESPONSIBILITIES OF WIVES

> *Your wife is your most important partner in life, your soulmate, your teammate, your prime root, and most importantly, she is the same as you.*

Living in fear of her husband

The Bible says that fear has torment. Under no circumstances should anyone live in fear. Anyone can be unhealthy in an environment that makes them fearful. No husband should use coercion to force his wife to submit. Submission obtained by coercion is not submission. Coercion into compliance with the toxic spirit of bullying and intimidation is what I call it.

So, what really is submission?

According to Oxford online, submission can be expressed this way:

It is the action or fact of accepting or yielding to the will or authority of another person.

The keywords in this definition are: *"accepting," "yielding," and "will" or "headship"*

This simply means the Bible asks that wives recognize, accept, or yield to their husbands' authority. It also means that the wife overtly chooses not to resist or oppose her husband's will. The only exception to this is that she's not expected to follow him to do something that is biblically incorrect or forbidden by law. Now, it is important to understand that the Bible is not saying anything new. We all submit to others almost daily. Can't you see yourself in this definition when you go to work?

MARITAL RESPONSIBILITIES OF WIVES

Unless you are no longer interested in your job, you submit to your boss at work, whether consciously or unconsciously. You're probably out of that position if you can show that you don't recognize your boss' authority over you.

Have you not realized how benign the word "submission" is? Therefore, I wonder why submission seems to have become such a distasteful word to many these days regarding family relationships. It is not helpful to take submission out of context or give it a different meaning than what Paul was inspired to write concerning marriage.

From a biblical standpoint, submission means, the wife

- recognizes the husband's headship over her.
- unconditionally respects her husband.

Therefore, submission is the unique biblical command whereby the wife recognizes and affirms her husband's headship over her so that together, they can lead a blissful, high-functioning, stable family life and ultimately fulfill God's purpose for their lives as a couple.

The importance of being under authority

Being under authority is never a bad thing. In fact, from my personal experience, I can state without fear of contradiction that being under authority is a blessing. Therefore, a woman who recognizes and deliberately affirms her husband's authority is well-positioned to reap the full benefits of being under authority.

MARITAL RESPONSIBILITIES OF WIVES

I find that there are several benefits to being under authority. For instance, when you are under authority, all the heavy lifting is usually done by the authority and not by those beneath it. That heavy lifting can be in the form of decision-making.

The decision-maker does most of the thinking, and he is aware that he will be held totally responsible for any decisions that result in a negative outcome. This is why responsible leaders often share their positive outcomes with everyone during their term but are gracious enough to accept full responsibility for anything that did not go as planned. Those in positions of authority are fully aware of how unpleasant it is to live with a decision that results in a negative outcome.

In this regard, I've seen some women in power struggle with their husbands make terrible blunders. Some women literally make a mess and then turn to their husbands for assistance in cleaning it up. When I witness such a situation, I'm tempted to think that God allows such bad outcomes as a painful lesson for wives who try to distort God's ordained order in the home.

Another benefit of being under authority is the blessing of those under it. In a home, that responsibility lies with the husband, and the blessed recipients will be the wife and her children. The easiest and most likely way to reject your husband's blessing is to disparage him by rejecting his authority over you. It is a spiritual fact of life that if you disparage anyone's authority, you will automatically reject the blessings that are supposed to come from that person.

MARITAL RESPONSIBILITIES OF WIVES

> A woman who recognizes her husband's authority is well-positioned to reap the full benefits of being under a responsible authority.

The actual implication of not yielding to the husband's authority in the home is that two captains are piloting such a family. And it is a well-known fact that any ship that two captains are piloting is inevitably sailing towards a disastrous end. For this reason, there should be no ambiguity about the order of authority in the home.

> And it is a well-known fact that any ship that two captains are piloting is inevitably sailing towards a disastrous end.

Unconditional submission from the wife

"Now I praise you, brethren, that you remember me in all things and keep the traditions just as I delivered them to you. But I want you to know that the head of every man is Christ, the head of woman is man, and the head of Christ is God" (1 Corinthians 11:2-3).

"Wives, submit to your own husbands, as to the Lord. For the husband is head of the wife, as also Christ is head of the church; and He is the Savior of the body. Therefore, just as the church is subject to Christ, so let the wives be to their own husbands in everything" (Ephesians 5:22-24).

Just as there is an unambiguous biblical requirement for husbands to love their wives to death unconditionally, so is the requirement for submission for wives. As I said earlier, the wife

MARITAL RESPONSIBILITIES OF WIVES

does not have to earn her husband's affection. Similarly, the husband does not need to earn his wife's submission. As a result, the wife should not impose any conditions on the husband for her to submit to him. That, I believe, is a divine proposition that is both fair and balanced.

> *Just as there is an unambiguous biblical requirement for husbands to love their wives to death unconditionally, so is the requirement for submission for wives.*

Ted and Veren's story

During the crash in the price of crude oil and gas, circa mid-2015, I heard something that stunned me. This brilliant mid-career engineer, Ted, lost his high-paying job in Canada's oil patch sector. He remained unemployed for over two years, despite his aggressive search for a new opportunity. As a result, Ted's personal financial situation became very precarious.

In the meantime, his wife, Veren, was working and earning a six-figure salary. Strangely, she started behaving unruly towards her husband. The situation degenerated to the point that Veren started hanging out with her unmarried friends in places where she would ordinarily be out of place. The situation was brought to our attention, and when we sought to know what in the world was going on, she arrogantly responded, "Ted and I have switched roles at the moment."

I asked her what she meant by that. She said, "Well, it is the person that pays the bills that is the boss. So, since I am the one paying all the bills in the house, I have the right to do what the

MARITAL RESPONSIBILITIES OF WIVES

boss is supposed to be doing, including going wherever my heart pleases. Once Ted gets a job, our traditional roles in the house will be restored. He will be the boss again. But until then, I am as free as the air to go wherever I choose. After all, I am the one sustaining the family at this time," she defiantly concluded.

It is somewhat unusual to hear something so bizarre. The wife should not submit to her husband only if the husband is paying the bills. Although bill payment is important, it is not what grants the husband default authority in the home. According to the scriptural provision, he has such authority merely because he is the husband.

And naturally, most men inherently understand and accept this responsibility whole-heartedly. Only a very small number of men will happily abdicate their responsibility of providing for their family to their wives. Most husbands can do anything legitimate to earn money to provide for their families.

Russell and Jennifer's story

I was told of a decent gentleman who demonstrated such responsibility to the amazement of everyone, including his wife. A number of years ago, Russell was suddenly laid off from his high-profile job with one of the leading commercial banks in his country. He felt so ashamed about the situation that he had no courage to tell his wife, Jennifer. After mulling over what had just happened to him, Russell determined that informing his wife about it was unnecessary.

However, he swiftly devised a strategy. Every morning, in the months following his job loss, Russell would dress up just like he always did as a banker and leave the house at the same time

MARITAL RESPONSIBILITIES OF WIVES

he used to. This time, the only difference was that he would drive his car out to provide taxi services to commuters. It's worth noting that, in Russell's part of the world, driving a taxi was not a particularly well-regarded type of work, especially for a university-educated professional. Also, there was no such thing as Uber by this time, which has elevated commercial driving to a whole new level.

Jennifer's friend Phoebe observed him stop and pick up passengers on multiple occasions. Phoebe became curious after seeing Russell pick up and drop off passengers regularly and decided to ask Jennifer about Russell's job situation.

Phoebe tactfully asked Jennifer: "Is everything okay with Russell's job at all?"

Jennifer answered in the affirmative and then continued, "He went to work even today. Why do you ask?"

Phoebe told Jennifer, "I have seen Russell using his car for taxi services on several occasions, even during business hours when he is supposed to be in the office. Maybe you should ask him what's really going on," she suggested.

When Russell got home in the evening that same day, Jennifer asked him the usual question wives ask their husbands after work.

"How was work today?"

"Fine," Russell answered his wife.

"Are you sure? You look exhausted."

MARITAL RESPONSIBILITIES OF WIVES

"As you know, no two days in the life of a banker are the same," Russell said in defense.

Jennifer said, "Anyway, somebody called to tell me that she has been seeing you use your car to pick up and drop off passengers. According to her, she has seen you do this repeatedly, and she decided to ask me what was going on with your job. Please, tell me, is everything alright with your job?"

Then Russell opened up to his wife, "Hmmm, actually, something happened at work."

"I am listening. What happened?" Jennifer asked.

"I lost my job a couple of months ago."

Jennifer was upset to hear this from her husband. She further asked him,

"Why did you hide such a significant event from me? I am very disappointed in you, Russell. You know that I am earning well. You know that we can conveniently survive on my earnings for some time while we keep trusting God to open another door for you."

Russell calmly responded, "I did not know how to break such bad news to you. I was so distraught and ashamed that I decided to keep it to myself." He continued, "but as the head of my family, I have decided to do whatever it takes to provide for you and the kids. As you know me quite well, I am always driven by the Word of God. I am acutely aware of what First Timothy 5:8 says, that '… if anyone does not provide for his own, and

MARITAL RESPONSIBILITIES OF WIVES

especially for those of his household, he has denied the faith and is worse than an unbeliever.'"

He went further, saying, "It is true your friend saw me. I have been using my car for taxi services over the past several weeks, but I am sure it will be okay soon. I am actively applying for open positions. God will soon open another door for us."

That's the extent some husbands can go to demonstrate their commitment and a sense of responsibility to their families.

Rod and Cassie's story

Cassie was very enthusiastic about spiritual matters. Her passion for working with children was infectious, making her a significant part of our new church plant. On the other hand, her husband, Rod, was the direct opposite. He wouldn't have anything to do with God or the church. Cassie will prepare breakfast for her husband, get ready, and leave for church every Sunday morning. Rod will not eat his food.

After service, Cassie will come home to find the food just like she served it, and she will ask her husband, "Rod, you didn't eat your food. What happened?" Rod will answer Cassie, "Don't be stupid! Who did you keep that cold food for? As you know quite well, I don't eat cold food." Cassie will answer, "But you know that I will be late to church if I have to wait for you to eat. The microwave is there. You could have warmed it." Rod will nag, bad mouth, and defame his wife until he has no strength in him. Cassie was well aware that Rod was doing everything he could to prevent her from attending church.

MARITAL RESPONSIBILITIES OF WIVES

Cassie endured her husband's abusive behavior until she decided that she has had enough of it. At that point, she determined in her heart that she would rebel against Rod and let him do his worst. But before going all out with her rebellion, she decided to talk to me about her intentions. I took the time to explain the spiritual implications of rebellion. I assured her that rebellion would only worsen the already bad situation.

> I told her the implications of rebellion. I assured her that rebellion will only worsen the already bad situation.

I also used the opportunity to explain to her that as difficult as it seemed, Rod was her immediate mission field. Most mission fields are usually treacherous. I told her that God was counting on her to bring her husband to the saving knowledge of Jesus. My counsel was a bit of a hard sell for Cassie, but she managed to take it gracefully.

In addition, I used the opportunity to explain to her what the Bible says about spousal relationships, that, "Wives, fit in with your husbands' plans; for then if they refuse to listen when you talk to them about the Lord, they will be won by your respectful, pure behavior. Your godly lives will speak to them better than any words." (1 Peter 3:1-2)

I advised her to maintain self-control and patience with Rod. Before she left for church, I told her to always wait for her husband to finish his breakfast. For the sake of her marriage, I told her it was fine if she arrived late to church. That way, she could have made her husband happy while still coming to

MARITAL RESPONSIBILITIES OF WIVES

church. We were also praying for Cassie while she was going through her ordeal.

She reluctantly followed my counsel. For the next several months that followed, she would stay behind for her husband to eat his breakfast before coming to church. After doing this consistently for about six months, Rod was touched. First, he started allowing her to set the table and leave for church. After about a year, Rod started attending church. One Saturday evening, I visited the family and thanked Rod for coming to church with them. He then opened up to me and acknowledged that his wife had shown that her marriage comes before church, and that's why he had decided to follow her to church.

Isn't that God's intervention co-mingled with wisdom and shrewdness? It's important to realize that Cassie did not become less important in the process as a wife. Rather, she made a significant impact on her husband by prioritizing her marriage. She eventually won her husband's heart, and as a result, he became a Christian. Rod went from being a mean and passionate God-hater to becoming a changed man. Their marriage found peace, and they both became devout Christians. Women who understand men know just how easy most of them are to deal with, especially in a marriage relationship.

> *Women who understand men know just how easy they are to deal with, especially in a marriage relationship.*

Of course, your experience may not be the same as Cassie's. However, there are some fine lessons in her story that we can all learn from. It makes it more interesting when the wife is dealing

MARITAL RESPONSIBILITIES OF WIVES

with an unsaved or agnostic spouse. The most important lesson is to see your home as a mission field with your spouse as your potential convert. In such situations, I find that a prayerful, calm, wise, patient and gentle approach will work almost all the time. Proverbs 16 says that from a wise mind comes wise speech; the words of the wise are persuasive. Kind words are like honey, which is sweet to the soul and healthy for the body (Proverbs 16:23-24).

KEY TAKE AWAY

- The following situations are not a lack of submission from the wife:
    - Attempt to be a positive influence on the husband.
    - The wife tactfully helps the husband to see different viewpoints when making an important decision.
    - Wife's refusal to keep quiet in the face of domestic violence or abuse.
    - Wife's refusal to cave into her husband's control.
- Biblical submission simply means that the wife recognizes her husband's authority over her.
- The wife's submission can help to boost the husband's self-esteem.
- The wife's submission brings peace and stability to the home environment.
- A marriage that is fashioned after God's order is characterized by:
    - Peace, tranquility, and stability.
    - Unbreakable bonding and unity between the husband and his wife.

- Attracting God's blessings. Psalms 133 tells us that where there is unity, God commands the abiding of his blessings. In other words, God is under obligation to release his blessings to any organization or institution where the people involved are operating in unity. Your family will greatly benefit from staying glued together.

- Fruitfulness and fulfillment in every area of the family's endeavor.

CHAPTER NINE

WIFE'S CHEERLEADING HER HUSBAND

Cheerleading is an activity in which the participants (called "cheerleaders") cheer for their team as a form of encouragement or motivation. The act of cheerleading includes anything from chanting slogans to engaging in strenuous physical activity. Usually, cheerleading is done to motivate sports teams, entertain the audience, and compete, or a combination of these three things.

Cheerleading is an important responsibility because it plays a critical role in ensuring the success of the team that is being cheered. Cheerleading creates a bond between the team and the fans. The crowd's energy and enthusiasm of the cheering crowd can motivate a sports team, boost their overall morale for optimal performance, and ultimately help them win the game.

To be effective, cheerleaders need to have a high endurance threshold to lead the fans until the end of the game. A high endurance threshold is required because the cheerleading role is often needed most when the team is not performing as well as it should. Anyone will make a very good use of cheerleading, particularly when morale is low. When things aren't going as smoothly as they should be, cheerleading comes in handy.

MARITAL RESPONSIBILITIES OF WIVES

As I have interacted with women from different socio-cultural backgrounds and educational levels, I've realized that almost all of them have one common and fascinating expectation. Most married women expect their husbands to be confident goal-getters who will go out into the world and conquer it, while many are content with playing a supporting role to their husbands.

Let me state here that cheerleading should play a significant role in that support role. Let me also be quite clear about something. I'm not proposing that wives be relegated to the cheerleader role. I'm just saying that I've heard many women remark that they would prefer to be on the sidelines cheering on their husbands to succeed rather than being on the field themselves playing.

When it comes to cheering, a man's thirst for it is almost unquenchable. It is not, however, their fault. That's precisely how God designed them. No wonder most men tend to gravitate towards the direction where cheering for them is loudest.

> Every married woman expects her husband to be a confident, goal-getter, confident, and competent to be able to go out into the world and conquer it.

Wives who clearly understand their cheerleading role and its impact usually leverage it to boost their husbands' morale. Wives can use it to keep their husbands inspired to go out there and conquer the world. More so, the husband can take advantage of his wife's cheerleading duties at any time, especially when his morale is down.

MARITAL RESPONSIBILITIES OF WIVES

> *No wonder men tend to gravitate towards the direction where cheering for them is loudest.*

Persistence in Cheerleading

Cheerleading doesn't stop until the game is over. Therefore, no matter how poorly your husband may be doing at the moment, please don't give up on him because I can assure you that his game of life is still very much on. As her husband's cheerleader, the wife's goal is to keep cheering him on until he achieves the much-desired victory.

Cheerleaders love and value their team regardless of whether they win or not. Correspondingly, the team feels appreciated and valued when they are persistently cheered on. That's what drives them to victory. Therefore, wives, you've got to keep cheering on your husbands until they become successful in their life's endeavors!

How to Cheer for your Husband

The wife can cheer on her husband with words such as, "Go, Honey, Go! You are doing well. Keep going. I have your back! I know you can do it." She can also praise him for whatever he does for the family, no matter how small. You can praise his big and not-so-big accomplishments at work and at home. Don't miss the opportunity to announce his successes to relevant people, such as friends and extended family members. Let the children know that their dad is a wonderful man. Never, ever, put him down in front of the kids, or anybody else for that matter.

MARITAL RESPONSIBILITIES OF WIVES

If you are somebody's wife and you are wondering if such simple words will make any difference, I will say emphatically that yes, such kind and inspiring words are essential and will go a long way in lifting him up until he turns the corner. The words may sound simple, but they have incredible spirit-lifting power. Use them liberally and be genuine when using them. They can make your husband want to come home after each day's work or to go out and seek opportunities that would give him a sense of purpose and significance.

> Let the children know that their dad is a great man.

Consequences of Grumbling

Wives should ensure that grumbling and complaining are eliminated from their marital relationships because they generate a depressing atmosphere. Grumbling consumes away positive energy and establishes the spirit of defeat wherever it is widespread, whereas cheerleading boosts morale and lifts spirits.

There is a saying that you do not kick a man who is already down. This means that when your husband is down, he needs a helping hand that lifts him up so he can stand. The least of what he needs is grumbling and demeaning him. When a wife grumbles at her husband's temporary setbacks, she effectively kicks him or makes him feel defeated in life.

In his first letter to the Corinthians, Paul admonished them not to grumble as the children of Israel did, for which many were destroyed (1 Corinthians 10:10). And in his letter to the church at Ephesus, he penned these words: "Don't use unwholesome or foul language. Let everything you say be good and helpful

MARITAL RESPONSIBILITIES OF WIVES

so that your words will be an encouragement to those who hear them" (Ephesians 4:29). Obviously, Paul's advice against grumbling and complaining is probably most relevant in a marital relationship than anywhere else.

> When a wife grumbles at her husband's temporary setbacks, she effectively kicks him or even crushes him to death.

Wife's Cheerleading Her Husband

KEY TAKE AWAY

It is important for wives to carefully note the following:

- The wife and her husband both share a responsibility to make their marriage stable and flourish, which is important for the whole family to thrive. Your children will thank you both for it.

- Your husband will NOT become a better person simply because he has endured constant criticism from you.

- Your husband will be grateful for your genuine praise of his efforts.

- A combination of respect, prayers, affirmation of him and his strengths will make him a model husband and father of your children.

- No one enjoys being nagged at. Remember, a joyful, cheerful heart brings healing to both the body and the soul. But the one whose heart is crushed struggles with sickness and disease.

- No one should be so heartless to still kick someone who is already down. Therefore, what a low-achieving and down-cast husband needs from you, his wife, is to cheer him back to his feet.

PART FOUR

Areas of Mutual Responsibility

- Chapter Ten: Mutual Marital Responsibilities
- Chapter Eleven: Respect
- Chapter Twelve: Prioritization
- Chapter Thirteen: Support
- Chapter Fourteen: Care, Provision and Protection
- Chapter Fifteen: Partnership
- Chapter Sixteen: Sexual Intimacy
- Chapter Seventeen: Bequeath Legacies

"An enemy might be able to defeat one person, but two people can stand back-to-back to defend each other. And three people are even stronger. They are like a rope that has three parts wrapped together—it is very hard to break" (Ecclesiastes 4:12 ERV).

CHAPTER TEN

MUTUAL MARITAL RESPONSIBILITIES

In this part, we'll look at the areas of marriage where the husband and wife both have a shared responsibility for their marriage to thrive.

The golden rule

"Do unto others as you would have them do unto you" is a biblical concept taught by Jesus and is found in Mathew 7:12 and Luke 6:31. This is a teaching most of us received from our parents early in our childhood.

But let's take a close look at this rule for a moment.

Would this rule be sufficient and beneficial in our post-modern culture, where autonomy and individualism are encouraged and even celebrated?

If we limit ourselves to this rule as we seek to build good interpersonal relationships, we would essentially be treating others the way we want to be treated and not necessarily the way they would wish to be treated.

According to Gary Chapman, author of The Five Love Languages, it is generally known and accepted by many that

AREAS OF MUTUAL RESPONSIBILITY

love and respect can be expressed to others in one or more of these five important ways:

- *words of affirmation*
- *spending quality time together*
- *acts of service*
- *giving gifts*
- *appropriate physical touch*

Not very long ago, while having coffee with a colleague, she told me that she is one of those people that does not identify being loved and cared for with acts of service.

That means that a person whose love language is *serving*, for example, may feel that serving is a manifestation of their affection and dedication to which they have dedicated time and effort and that serving will demonstrate their affection and dedication to the receiver. "While I would certainly appreciate such a gesture, "acts of service" is my least proficient love language and does not communicate the message of love based on my preferences," she added.

"Though being served by someone who likes to serve can be a nice idea, it does not necessarily show me that they know me; it only shows me that they know themselves, as they are obviously doing what comes naturally to them," she concluded. Her exception piqued my interest, and it made me ponder. But of course, that is who she is as a unique individual.

It's difficult to fathom how we would be able to form intimate and wholesome relationships if we all treated people the way we want to be treated. We must appreciate that various people have different values, perspectives, and even cultural beliefs that impact how they wish to be treated while striving to develop wholesome relationships. For instance, you can have a forthright friend who values raw honesty, but you might also have a more sensitive friend who requires softer words. Would you treat them the same way?

I recall a not-so-interesting encounter my son and I had with an acquaintance during a parent-teacher conference at my son's school some years ago. We came across a gentleman who, according to him, was originally from one of the West African countries. My son, who was about fourteen years old at the time and entirely oblivious to this man's cultural peculiarities, extended his hand to shake him. The man was furious, and he began to wonder aloud what type of child my son was to be so impolite to extend his hand to shake him, a much older person.

I reminded the gentleman that I do not share the same cultural values as him, hence the difference in how I raise my children. My son found the man's behavior strange, but I took the time to educate him about the man's background.

In fact, my son was practicing what he had been taught as a Canadian social way of life. The gentleman was expecting something completely different. What a huge disconnect and misapplication of our effort if we treat others the way we want to be treated.

As a result of the foregoing, we can see why we should center deeply our relationships on what the specific person we care about actually needs rather than what we require. This means that cherishing your spouse necessitates considering their unique preferences and recognizing what makes them feel special. This is critical because successful relationships require

AREAS OF MUTUAL RESPONSIBILITY

knowledge and consideration of the other person beyond our own self-understanding.

> What a huge potential disconnect and misapplication of our effort if we treat others the way we want to be treated.

Therefore, the challenge in today's world demands more than the golden rule. That is, realizing that what is best for us is not always the best for other people because what is best for us may simply be the very basic expectation for others. That means that it is important for us to strive to know our spouses thoroughly, show them the affection they would like to receive in their own unique way, and treat them the way they would like to be treated.

Kevin and Amber's story

Over the past several months, I have had a series of fence-mending discussions with a couple whose marriage was less than a year old. The husband, Kevin, loves to cook. And in his unique way of showing affection to his wife, Kevin took charge of the kitchen and would cook for his wife, Amber.

During one of our therapy sessions, Kevin took time to tell me, in the presence of his wife, how he had been doing his best to show his wife the depth of his love for her. Then he narrated how he does all the cooking as well as cleaning. Amber quickly interjected and told her husband to stop wasting his time. She asked Kevin, "Who asked you to be the cook of the house?" She continued, "Your cooking doesn't mean anything to me." Kevin was shocked to hear this from his wife.

AREAS OF MUTUAL RESPONSIBILITY

Couples, you will be wise if you can take the time to get to know your spouse well enough to love him or her in the most appropriate way and stop misdirecting your efforts. Your effort will be much more effective if you can love him or her from their perspective and not based on what you think is best for them.

Thus, in putting spousal relationships into perspective, we can benefit from what Apostle Peter wrote (already discussed in chapter three above) about husbands dwelling with their wives according to knowledge. As we discuss these areas of mutual responsibility, I will invite couples to step outside of their bubble and start treating their spouse the way they want to be treated.

Husbands must make the necessary effort to get to know their wives to be better positioned to treat them accordingly. In the exact same way, wives must make the necessary effort to get to know their husbands so that they can give their husbands their preferred treatment.

The responsibilities I have identified below as being mutual are the responsibilities that both the husband and the wife are expected to fulfill towards each other. And as in all other areas of responsibility already discussed in Parts Two and Three above, each partner should take them seriously and do them as faithfully as possible.

I have purposely repeated myself quite a few times that marriage is a spiritual undertaking which is meant for mature adults, and the required behavior to hold a marriage together must also be mature. Obviously, such repetition is for the sake of emphasis.

KEY TAKE AWAY

- Although the golden rule is essential and has a place in building interpersonal relationships, you will need to do more than what the rule says in pursuit of a high-functioning marriage.

- You will need to go a lot deeper to thoroughly understand your spouse before you can love and respect them in their own unique way.

- It will not be the best use of your effort to work so hard to impress your spouse based on your assumption of what you think they will like. Dig deeper and know what makes them truly happy.

CHAPTER ELEVEN

RESPECT

Respect, also called esteem, is a positive feeling or action shown towards someone or something considered important or held in high esteem or regard. Respect conveys a sense of admiration for good or valuable qualities. Respecting or highly esteeming your spouse is crucial in a marriage that will thrive over the long term because we all appreciate it when we are treated with respect. As a result, both the husband and the wife must demonstrate respect towards each other. The husband esteems his wife in the same way that the wife esteems her husband. Mutual respect is necessary for any marriage seeking to be or is already regarded as high-functioning.

Holding someone in high esteem is an excellent morale-boosting trick. When we are treated with respect, we tend to be at our best—our spirits are high, we feel good about ourselves, and our confidence level is elevated. When we are well-regarded by others around us, the best in us emerges naturally. Nobody wants to be rejected or treated as a non-entity. Understandably, when it comes from one's own spouse, the awful feeling of being treated disrespectfully worsens.

AREAS OF MUTUAL RESPONSIBILITY

> *When we are treated with respect, we tend to be at our best—our spirits are high, we feel good about ourselves, and our confidence level is elevated.*

The benefits of respect in marriage

Here are some of the practical ways your marriage stands to gain when you treat your spouse with respect.

Satisfaction in marriage

In a marriage where there is mutual respect, couples feel a great sense of connectedness to their spouse and their overall marital experience in general. They feel that they are part of something very special. It makes each spouse feel desired. Respect makes how we fit into the grand scheme of things more obvious.

Respectful behaviour can lift spirits and brighten one's otherwise difficult day. Treating your spouse with respect can instil confidence in them and offer them much-needed inspiration. Consequently, couples who experience a deep sense of respect also report greater satisfaction in their married life. The opposite is also true: couples report more conflicts and misunderstandings in marriages where there is little or no respect. Affected couples feel trampled upon, unimportant, and even irrelevant.

> *Couples who experience a deep sense of respect, also report greater satisfaction in their married life.*

AREAS OF MUTUAL RESPONSIBILITY

Increases partners' engagement

It is nearly impossible to overemphasize the fact that respect is a powerful force. For instance, attaining one hundred percent employee engagement in the business world is an ambitious target all organizations would love to reach. Many organizations, in fact, consider respect to be one of their core values and, consequently, devote a significant portion of their resources in pursuit of this target.

Unfortunately, a recent Gallup study of over 350,000 American employees in different organizations revealed that only a paltry 30% reported real engagement with their work. In addition to other common strategies for inspiring disengaged employees, experience also shows that one of the proven strategies is for managers and senior leaders themselves to show respect for their employees. That's what is called "leading by example."

Furthermore, in another survey of more than 20,000 employees, Harvard Business Review found that respect was the number one behavior, above all others, that would lead to greater employee engagement and commitment. Employees reported that respect from their managers, including senior leaders, had a more significant positive impact on them than useful feedback, recognition, sharing the company vision, or even opportunities for personal and career development. Respect is that important to us human beings.

Although the above workplace scenarios depict an employee-employer relationship, they do highlight what is intrinsically vital to us as humans, regardless of the setting in which we find ourselves. I must stress that the unique relationship we have in a marriage setting positions us to set a much higher bar than in

AREAS OF MUTUAL RESPONSIBILITY

any other type of relationship. That's why couples must actively leverage this understanding to stimulate an unbeatable sense of engagement in their partner's life and marriage.

> I must stress that the unique relationship we have in a marriage setting positions us to set a much higher bar than the norm.

Respect alleviates stress

In trying to understand how respect alleviates stress in a marriage, let me once again draw a parallel with what happens in a typical work environment. Many workplace studies have consistently shown that a respected employee no longer has reason to fear being stepped on or stepped over by anyone. As a result, he or she doesn't have the stress experienced by employees who don't receive the same respect.

The respected person is also at ease enough to be themselves and live and work within their own skin without the stress of feeling they have to impress everyone around them. They don't have to put up with the stress of pretending to be someone they are not. That's precisely what happens when your spouse enjoys your respect. He or she is composed, relaxed, confident, emotionally and psychologically stable, knowing that he or she will not be treated like a stranger who is not known to do anything well.

How to show respect to your spouse

It has been said that respect is something one needs to earn; it's not something that's handed out freely on a golden platter. However, let me state here that your spouse has earned that

AREAS OF MUTUAL RESPONSIBILITY

respect simply by being your spouse. When you made the decision to choose them as your life partner, it meant that, in your eyes, you already respected them as a person, a future spouse, and the parent of your future children.

So, when you're married, if you ignore the respect you had for them initially and instead wait and watch how they would perform to determine your current respect for them, you're setting your marriage up for failure. Always know that your spouse is your all-around superstar and must be treated as such.

Your spouse earned the highest respect from you when you chose to make them your spouse, which means that every little accomplishment they attain from then on will only further confirm that they are the wonderful person God has blessed you with.

> Your spouse is your all-round superstar and must be treated as such.

Respect is a virtue that is best demonstrated and least imagined. That is to say, if we limit our respect to the realm of imagination, our intended recipient, our spouse, will not feel or experience it. As a result, we must demonstrate it, which we can do in various ways, including simply affirming our spouse. We must set aside our prejudices, pride, inflated egos, and self-centeredness in order to respect one another.

Be in full control of your words

One of the easiest and fastest ways to destroy a relationship is through our words. In helping couples to resolve their conflicts, I

AREAS OF MUTUAL RESPONSIBILITY

occasionally hear them utter despicable things about each other, and I'm baffled as to how individuals who share their intimate lives together can allow things to get to such an unfortunate level. Some couples come across as if they are competing to say the cruelest things to the other partner.

The marriage institution is not the place where couples can develop a sharp tongue so they can spew out such unwholesome words against each other. I advise warring couples to make every effort necessary to control their tongue, especially as they interact with each other. I find it rather strange that some couples are quick to admit that no marriage is perfect, thus giving tacit justification for their foul language and lack of effort to lead a healthier married life.

One of the very good ways to help us tame our tongue is to practice not using it in the first place. Stated differently, we should make more effort to listen, and listen more intently, which is what James said in his letter. He said, "So then, my beloved brethren, let every man be swift to hear, slow to speak, slow to wrath; for the wrath of man does not produce the righteousness of God" (James 1:19-20). This counsel is important because words often have a substantial impact, and sadly once something is said, it can't be taken back.

In the third chapter of his letter, James went further to say that we all stumble in many things. If anyone does not stumble in word, he is a perfect man, and such a person is also able to control the whole body. And Proverbs eighteen says that death and life are in the power of the tongue, and those who love it will eat its fruit (Proverbs 18:21).

AREAS OF MUTUAL RESPONSIBILITY

According to these Bible verses, we demonstrate our perfection mainly in our capacity for wise and careful usage of our tongue. Proverbs ten says, "In the multitude of words sin is not lacking, but he who restrains his lips is wise" (Proverbs 10:19). That is, the one who talks much will for sure sin, but he who is careful in what he says is wise. And in Ecclesiastes, we learn that "… a fool's voice is known by multitude of words" (Ecclesiastes 5:3).

These verses invariably say that you come across as foolish when you talk without exercising self-control. In other words, it is important to think carefully before speaking. If you don't, you will keep causing great damage to your relationships, including your marriage. These Bible passages also encourage us to learn to choose our words wisely so that we'll be well on our way to building a healthy marriage. Conversely, you will easily destroy your marriage by being carelessly mouthy.

> *Choose your words wisely and carefully, and you will be well on your way to building a healthy marriage.*

For example, in the heat of their marital conflict, an otherwise pleasant young woman referred to her mother-in-law as a witch. Unfortunately, that proved to be the final straw that broke the camel's back. Following that remark, the husband makes it clear that he will not forgive a wife who refers to his mother as a witch. He divorced her as a result and has since remarried.

> *The one who talks much will surely sin, but he who is careful in what he says is wise.*

AREAS OF MUTUAL RESPONSIBILITY

Communication experts suggest that to improve your active listening skills, the next time you're in a conversation, you repeat, in your mind, every word the other person says. It takes time to master the skill, but it is well worth the effort. This technique has two major benefits. When you mentally repeat a speaker's every word, they will notice and appreciate that you intently listen and show respect for them.

This technique also forces you to really focus on what the speaker is saying, so you can't think about what you will say next. When you listen attentively to someone speaking, you're being respectful of them and they will, in return, respect you for that. Careful listeners naturally earn the respect of others to whom they listen.

> *It is important to think carefully before speaking. Otherwise, you will keep causing great damage to your relationship, including marriage.*

Empathize

Empathy is the ability to experience and relate to the thoughts, emotions, or experiences of others. Empathy is also the ability to step into someone else's shoes, be aware of their feelings, and understand their needs. It is distinct from sympathy, which is the ability to support others with compassion.

When you empathize with your spouse's experience, you can better show respect toward them. Having extensively used empathy in my interpersonal relationships, I can say without a fear of contradiction that empathy can fuel an intense connection between individuals. This is true both for the giver

AREAS OF MUTUAL RESPONSIBILITY

as well as the receiver. On the other hand, a lack of empathy creates a disconnection between people in a relationship.

In conclusion, let me encourage you to try these simple interpersonal relationship-building techniques and watch your marriage blossom: say good morning to your spouse with whom you slept in the same bed, and be intentional about it. Also, be intentional about actively listening to your spouse every day. Encourage, assist, or comfort him or her as the need arises. Imbibe the very basics of greeting one another, pitching in to help when the other needs it, and giving each other space when required. Simply being kind is another important way of showing respect.

KEY TAKE AWAY

- Mutual respect is necessary in any marriage seeking to be or is already regarded as high-functioning.

- When we are treated with respect, we tend to be at our best – our spirits are high, we feel good about ourselves, and our confidence level is elevated.

- The awful feeling that comes with being treated disrespectfully tends to worsen when it happens in a marital relationship.

- Respect significantly contributes to;

    - Satisfaction in marriage

    - Spousal engagement

    - Alleviation of stress

- Your spouse has earned your respect simply for being your spouse. Don't wait for them to prove themselves before they can earn your respect.

- Respect for your spouse can be shown by being:

    - thoughtful in all your utterances and interactions

    - intentionally empathetic

- Nourish your spouse and marriage by routinely doing the following:
  - Say good morning to your spouse every morning
  - Encourage, assist, and comfort your spouse when needed
  - Give him or her space when required
  - Be intentionally kind to each other

CHAPTER TWELVE

PRIORITIZATION

At the heart of the Christian marital relationship is "leave and cleave" to form a union that will last for a lifetime until death forces the couple to separate. It is for this reason that the man will leave his father and mother and be joined to his wife, and they will become one flesh. This is according to Genesis 2:24. There is no other person in the whole world that is spiritually one flesh with you except your spouse. That is why your spouse must be the most important human being in your life.

For the sake of marriage, women often leave a lot behind. For example, women sometimes leave their cultural upbringing and even their country of birth because of marriage. And they usually do this quite joyfully. Isn't it reasonable to assume that something important enough to cause you to leave so much behind should also be the most important thing in your life?

To create a balance in the marriage process, God commands the man to reciprocate his wife's sacrifice by leaving his father and mother so that he can truly be joined to his wife. This "leaving" must be both in letter and in spirit. That's the only foundation that guarantees that no other human being or situation comes before your spouse.

AREAS OF MUTUAL RESPONSIBILITY

How can a husband accord his wife the highest priority?

When you get married, there may be people in your past who still believe they should remain the highest priority in your life because they held this spot before your marriage. In such cases, you need to be clear that your marriage, and by extension, your wife, is now your highest priority. And if they remain ignorant, keep repeating this until it finally sinks in. Remember that you must establish strict limits so that such individuals understand that you are no longer the same son, brother, or uncle that you were before marriage.

Regrettably, some cultures encourage the kind of behavior whereby some relations are supposed to be recognized above the wife. In such cultures, the wife is required to accord every family member born prior to the wife's arrival with special honor and respect.

Such cultures embolden in-laws to be rude towards the new wife. And because it is the culture, the husband is expected to follow it. As a result, it will be necessary to inform such family members that, whoever they were to you before you married, such ties will have to be relegated to second place behind your wife. It is that simple but serious!

Genesis 2:24 makes the statement "that the man shall leave his father and mother and shall cleave to his wife and the two shall become one flesh." It is so foundational and important that it cannot be repeated too many times. The significance of that verse is shown in the way our Lord Jesus reiterated it in Matthew 19. Similarly, Paul also referred to it in Ephesians 5.

AREAS OF MUTUAL RESPONSIBILITY

This underscores the need for the couple to make every sacrifice necessary to protect their marriage's integrity and hallowedness.

Other areas of conflict

Another potential area of conflict is friends. It is true that your childhood friends are important to you. However, once you get married, you have to help them understand that your wife is now your number one priority. Of course, they are still your friends. However, on the priority scale, they rank below your wife. You can still spend an appropriate amount of time with them while being careful that you are no longer that single person they used to know. It will also be inappropriate for them to make those unannounced visits to your house as they used to. It is no longer just a house, but it is now your matrimonial home. And they have to respect that.

This area of friendship equally applies to wives as well. The wife must let her friends know that she is now a married woman, and consequently, her relationship priorities have changed. I cannot over-emphasize this point since women often tend to be very emotional about their fellow female friends.

Work and family

Sometimes, newly married men allow their careers to collide with their marriage. Allowing that to happen is not a wise idea. I've seen some marriages fall apart simply because the husband becomes engrossed in his work and unconsciously acts as if he has forgotten he's a married man.

AREAS OF MUTUAL RESPONSIBILITY

Sean and Dawn's story

The following conversation ensued between Sean and his wife Dawn. Their marriage was only about three years old. Sean was routinely working late hours in the office. On one of such evenings of coming home late, Dawn was waiting for him at the door. As soon as Sean stepped inside the house, out of frustration, Dawn asked him,

"Where are you coming from?"

"Where else? From work, of course," Sean replied.

"This late?" Dawn probed further.

"You know about that huge and complex project I am managing. I had to stay behind to prepare stakeholder communication which must go out tomorrow morning."

Dawn replied, "Look, I am getting tired of hearing about all this huge and complex project stuff that you keep talking about. At this point, I must tell you to think very carefully and choose between your family and your job."

Sean was stunned. He took a deep breath and then calmly responded by asking Dawn, "What in the world is your problem? I have been working so hard so that I can provide for you and our son. I feel so confused to hear you ask me to choose between my career and you."

Dawn responded, "Listen, Sean, do you think I care about all these material things around me as much as I care about concrete proof that I am the most important thing in your life?"

AREAS OF MUTUAL RESPONSIBILITY

She went further to say, "Don't forget that I am a human being with feelings and the ability to know where I stack up on your scale of priorities."

Dawn then calmly but firmly counseled her husband. "Just make sure that you are ordering your priorities right. You have clearly failed to realize how difficult it is for me to be home all day with Junior. If you continue to work long hours and still bring home more work, with little or no time for us to spend together, then I am not going to take that any further."

Sean and Dawn's story will likely sound familiar to many young couples. What good is it for you to lose the family you thought you were working so hard to provide for? Striking a proper balance between your marriage and your job solves this type of conflict. Make sure your wife doesn't get the impression that anything, including your career, comes before her. You will almost certainly be disappointed with the outcome!

> *What good is it for you to lose the family that you thought you were working so hard to provide for?*

Prioritization

Spousal relationships and mothers

Many of the marital conflicts I've known involving parents often revolve around the husband's mother. This is not entirely unexpected because boys (not in all cases, though) are generally known to form strong attachments to their moms, which makes some adapt slowly to their new status as married men.

It is usually a case of mixed emotions for many mothers. They are obviously ecstatic about their son's new family, but there is

AREAS OF MUTUAL RESPONSIBILITY

also jealousy that another woman has entered their son's life. As a result, the son must apply wisdom and maturity to deal with these emotions as they arise, using the scriptural injunction to "leave and cleave" as a guide. Let me be clear: leaving and cleaving does not imply that the son would completely abandon his parents and refuse to have anything to do with them. By doing so, the scripture will be taken out of context.

It's also important for wives to understand that even though they are their husbands' highest priority, this doesn't mean that their husbands wouldn't maintain a relationship with their birth family. Now, it's important to note that the highest priority doesn't mean you are the only priority as a wife. I am stressing this point because I am aware of many instances where some wives have tried to discourage their husbands from continuing to have a meaningful relationship with their birth family because they considered themselves the husband's only priority. This approach is ill-advised because we still need meaningful support structures around us even though we are married. And obviously, the most important source of such support is our family.

A newly married young man who was already grappling with the fairly common conflict between his wife and his mother once asked me if he was supposed to choose between his mom and wife. I told him that it was not a matter of choosing between the two. I helped him understand that his mother and his wife were both extremely important to him and should be treated as such. However, I went further to let him know that, according to the Word of God, his wife has to take first place in his life as a married man.

AREAS OF MUTUAL RESPONSIBILITY

> *However, I went further to let him know that, according to the Word of God, his wife has to take first place in his life as a married man.*

In reality, sound wisdom mandates that the son works as hard as possible to ensure that his bride is well-loved and accepted by his parents and other family members. I find that approach to work well as it ultimately removes potential causes of conflict between the wife and the in-laws.

It would be naive for anyone to underestimate the task of a wife settling down into a new family and getting to know the different personalities within it. It is the husband's responsibility to help create a safe and secure environment for his wife to settle in and thrive. Thus, I believe that the "leave and cleave" injunction is specific to husbands because it is necessary to make sure the wife feels as secure in the new family as possible.

I had a personal experience with this type of situation. I was once attracted to a pretty girl in my undergraduate days. Very early on in the relationship, I innocently started talking about my mom. My closeness to my mom was obvious to everyone that knew our family. I would tell her stories revealing what a wonderful woman my mother was.

I was simply being myself as a young adult at the time and inexperienced at dating. I had no inkling that this was irritating my friend. After hearing so much about my mom within only a few months of our relationship, my friend opened up to me by politely asking if it was okay for her to tell me something. I immediately obliged her, nervously wondering what that would be. She said, "My impression of you is that you come across as

Prioritization

AREAS OF MUTUAL RESPONSIBILITY

someone whose wife will have problems. I feel that you will prefer your mom to your wife."

I was so stunned to hear this from her. In fact, I was completely taken unawares by her assertion. I took time to assure her, "That's not going to be the case. I am only trying to get you acquainted with the dynamics of my family." Apparently, she was not very convinced as the relationship did not gain any traction.

Although this was unintentional, I was simply setting a tone very early on that my mom was very important to me. As I matured a bit more, I started praying very consistently that God would give me a wife who would have a good relationship with my mom as well as other members of my family. I knew that if such a healthy relationship existed, my mom would not feel the characteristic jealousy that is commonly known to define daughter-in-law and mother-in-law relationships.

> As I matured a bit more, I started praying very consistently that God would give me a wife who would have a good relationship with my mom, as well as other members of my family.

I am pleased to testify that God has faithfully answered my prayer, as my wife has embraced every member of my family wholeheartedly, and she has a very healthy relationship with every one of them. As a result, I've had no conflict to manage in that regard. My wife will have to tell, but I don't believe there was ever a moment when she doubted she was my number one priority.

AREAS OF MUTUAL RESPONSIBILITY

Honor your father and mother

Let's discuss what the Bible says about parents generally and how they should fit into your family as a couple. In Ephesians six, Paul echoes the fifth commandment, which says, "Honor your father and mother, which is the first commandment with promise: *that it may be well with you* and *you may live long on the earth*" (Ephesians 6:2-3, emphasis added).

God is not the author of confusion. Therefore, he cannot be asking us to honor our parents while at the same time asking us to leave all else and cleave to our wives. The two commands are meant to be obeyed. God wants us to honor our parents and still be able to "leave and cleave" to our wives. These two passages provide us with good examples of why it is very important to always take a balanced and holistic approach when studying the Word of God.

Ephesians 6 is a beautiful scripture because it is a commandment that comes with two significant promises. The two promises are that when we honor our parents, i) it will be well with us, and ii) we will enjoy a long life. It is important to stress that this commandment does not apply solely to adolescents, young adults, or singles. As long as our parents are alive, we must all strive to follow this commandment in our relationship with them.

These Bible verses invariably imply that how we manage the relationship with our parents demonstrates how far we can go in life. In other words, there is a direct correlation between the *quality of our success* in life and the way we manage our relationship with our parents. The promise also includes our longevity. Clearly, our Christian faith is so well-rounded if only

Prioritization

AREAS OF MUTUAL RESPONSIBILITY

we would all take the time to study and thoroughly understand what the Word of God teaches.

We aren't allowed to pick and choose some provisions of the Word of God and be completely faithful in doing them while ignoring other related provisions. We are required to leave all else and cleave to our spouses. However, we must continue to honor our parents with the appropriate level of effort. Both provisions are biblically sound and necessary for our well-being.

How to honor your parents

If you are reading this book and you are a Christian with Christian parents, I would strongly recommend that one of the most important ways to honor your parents is to remain in the faith and serve the Lord with your own family as faithfully as you can. For a Christian, there is almost no greater honor you can do your parents.

I know this because I have had cause to pray with parents whose children have walked away from the faith. While ministering to such parents, you can feel the palpable pain they are enduring. On the other hand, I have witnessed the unspeakable joy of parents who proudly talk about their children faithfully serving the Lord. I can see that it is human for parents to exude such joy knowing that they did not fail to raise God-fearing children. And no one should take this feeling for granted because if you are a Christian and you have children, it will be your turn to feel the way your parents feel about you.

AREAS OF MUTUAL RESPONSIBILITY

> *On the other hand, I have witnessed the unspeakable joy of parents who proudly talk about their children faithfully serving the Lord.*

Of course, you are not in the faith simply because of your parents. However, the expectation is that you have grown up to be fully persuaded of your Christian faith. Without a shred of doubt, you know that Jesus is the Way, the Truth, and the Life, and no one gets to the Father without him.

If your parents are not Christians, then, obviously, this aspect of honor (that is, remaining active in the faith) will not apply to them. However, you can still leverage this biblical command to honor them in many other ways that compellingly communicate the light and beauty of your Christian faith. Below are a few other examples as a guide.

You can honor your parents through periodic visits. Regardless of whether or not they are Christians, every parent will appreciate this. You can decide how frequently such visits should occur. If you reside in the same city as them, for example, at least once a week might do. Once every three to six months may be sufficient if they live in a different city.

There is no rule about the frequency. You are free to determine what is appropriate for you. And when you are not visiting, make sure you are regularly calling to check how they are doing. If you are not able to visit in person, you can take advantage of some of the commonly available technologies that make virtual meetings very easy these days—tools such as Zoom, Skype, Facetime, and many more.

Prioritization

AREAS OF MUTUAL RESPONSIBILITY

While going on such visits, remember to go with a gift. It doesn't have to be an expensive gift. You will know what they normally like. Remember, they may not need or expect the gifts. But you are doing it as an act of honor for them. Depending on their age and ability to travel, they would appreciate it if you could let them know that they are also welcome to visit your family.

Furthermore, many families have some traditions, such as making sure that the family comes together during Easter and Christmas. Make sure you continue to honor such traditions while they are still alive. Parents are generally ecstatic when children and grandchildren all come together during such times.

You should also make sure you remember their birthdays as well as their wedding anniversary. Those are significant dates that a family-oriented and caring child should never forget. You will make them feel special if you can organize nice celebrations during milestone dates such as birthdays and marriage anniversaries.

Remember, it'd be nice to do the same for your two families. For example, if you spent Easter with your parents, you may consider spending Christmas with your wife's parents or vice versa. These are only a few examples; there are many other creative ways to show honor to your parents.

KEY TAKE AWAY

- There should be no doubt in your spouse's mind that he or she is the most important human being in your life.

- Be careful not to create an impression that your career is more important to you than your marriage.

- Husbands have a special responsibility to create a conducive environment for their wives to settle and thrive in the new family.

- "Leaving and cleaving" to your wife does not mean abandoning your parents.

- You can honor your father and mother and still make it clear that your wife is your highest priority.

- Find some creative ways to honor your parents because it is the right thing to do, but also that your destiny is partly tied to how well you manage your relationship with them.

- For those with Christian parents, one of the most important ways to honor them is by actively remaining in the faith and raising your own family to be godly.

CHAPTER THIRTEEN

SUPPORT

From time to time, we all need support, in one form or another. This is especially true in our all-important marital relationships, where the couple spends twenty-four hours a day, seven days a week, year-in and year-out, living life together. In such a relationship, mutual support is certainly not just a luxury but an absolute necessity. This support must be in all areas of the couple's life. Personally, I humbly concede to having no clue how I'd get through each day without my wife's unwavering support.

To build a genuinely high-functioning marriage and even achieve a near-perfect home environment for yourself and your children, one of the important keys is avoiding being rigid about role delineation between you and your spouse. That is, it is hardly helpful for the wife to insist that something is the husband's responsibility while the husband is there insisting that it's not a man's duty but that of the wife. Such an attitude will breed unnecessary tension and friction in your marriage.

> *It is hardly helpful for the wife to insist that something is the husband's responsibility while the husband is saying that it's not a man's duty, but the woman's.*

AREAS OF MUTUAL RESPONSIBILITY

The Husband's Support Responsibilities

In virtually every aspect of family life, any wife will be glad for her husband's support. As a result, husbands who already actively support their wives at home, I can only join your wives in praising you and encouraging you to keep up the great work. For those men who are still unsure of why and how they may help their wives, here are some suggestions you can start with:

The husband can support his wife through educational or professional development. In the reality of today's world, the quest for educational or professional development is no longer a rarity among women. Most women desire to develop themselves just like their male counterparts. And to do that successfully, a married woman will undoubtedly need her husband's support.

This support can come in many ways, including such simple things as offering words of encouragement. In fact, we all need those encouraging words, especially when we are under pressure or when the reality around us contradicts what we expected. Encouraging words of affirmation such as:

- I know you can do it.
- I have no doubt in your abilities.
- You are almost through.

will go a long way towards reinforcing the resolve and confidence of your wife towards her set goals.

The husband can also support his wife by providing help with house chores. Wives greatly appreciate help with some of the basic chores that have been traditionally seen as feminine duties: chores such as doing dishes, doing laundry, emptying the dishwasher, cleaning washrooms, vacuuming the floor, or taking out the garbage. Sometimes, you can offer to cook or go out for dinner so that she can reserve the energy she would have expended on cooking to study or do some professional development work or simply just rest.

I recently heard a marriage counselor on a Miracle Channel TV program say something that men should seriously consider taking to heart. He said that wives greatly appreciate help with household tasks that men often regard as mundane. He further said that women actually place their husbands' help with house chores on par with foreplay. Help with house chores is very important to wives. Husbands, please, take note and help as much as you can.

Support

Another important support that a husband can give is in his wife's career. Depending on his background and experience, the husband may be his wife's most immediate informal career coach. This form of support might range from coaching her to develop or polish her interpersonal skills necessary for success in a corporate environment to helping to proofread and edit her job deliverables.

In addition, a savvy husband who understands his wife's skills and strengths might assist her in deciding on a career route or changing it. It's not unusual for a mentor to recommend a professional path based on their deep knowledge of their mentee's abilities. A thoroughbred husband can act as his wife's career mentor when appropriate.

The husband can also assist with extracurricular activities such as athletics, dancing, and music lessons for the kids. Some of these family activities are solely the wife's responsibility in some cultures. As a result, when a husband breaks free from such a cultural mindset and begins to offer the much-needed support, the positive impact on his wife and, ultimately, on his marriage can be immense.

The Wife's Support Responsibilities for her husband

On the other hand, husbands usually appreciate their wives' support when they can contribute meaningfully to the family's well-being, including finances. However, if the couple agrees that the wife can stay at home and raise children, that's awesome too. It's worth noting that in some households, the husband is the one who is the stay at home partner. And there's nothing wrong with that as long as they're both on the same page with it.

This kind of support is increasingly becoming the norm rather than the exception. The dispensation of a wife claiming very personal ownership of her earnings is speedily fading away. And husbands greatly appreciate such support when it is available. Just as Proverbs 31 says, the wife who fully supports her husband will fit well into the description of a virtuous wife.

> The dispensation of a wife claiming very personal ownership of her earnings is speedily fading away.

Joint Bank Account

The question of whether or not a couple should have a joint account is becoming more prevalent these days. As a result, the number of couples who have a joint account also appears to be rising. In that manner, neither spouse claims personal ownership of the money, but rather that it belongs to the family—" it is our money." Having said that, I am not in any way advocating for a couple to operate a joint account.

I have been asked more than a few times if couples are biblically required to operate a joint account, and my consistent answer is that it should be up to the couple. That's a decision that the couple should make based on their mutual agreement. Whatever their decision may ultimately be, they must make sure that money is not causing conflict between them. I strongly recommend that couples should always be on guard to make sure that money is only a blessing and not a tool to break up their marriage. And they should be accountable to each other for ensuring that money is truly a blessing to their marriage rather than a curse.

> I strongly recommend that couples should always be on guard to ensure that finance is only a blessing and not a tool to break up their marriage.

Furthermore, when making such an important decision about their finances whether to operate a joint account or not, neither spouse should be so selfish as to base their position on what they think will be their contribution to the joint account. Regardless of how large your paycheck is relative to what your spouse earns, don't allow that income differential to influence your decision. That would be selfish and near-sighted. Whether you operate a joint account or not, the godly attitude for a married couple should always be "it is our family's money" instead of "it's my money." Note the transition from *me, mine,* and *I* to *us, ours,* and *we*.

AREAS OF MUTUAL RESPONSIBILITY

As money is usually a main area of conflict between couples, I recommend that this topic be discussed and agreed upon early on during courtship. For example, right from the onset, my wife prefers to have her own separate account, but she is joined to mine, and I am perfectly fine with that. I am very delighted to say that money has never been, and never will be, an issue in our marriage.

KEY TAKE AWAY

- In marriage, mutual support is not just a luxury but an absolute necessity.

- Strict role delineation is antithetical to a healthy and high-functioning marriage.

- The husband can support his wife's educational and professional development through simple words of affirmation.

- Women are usually grateful when their husbands step in and support them with house chores such as doing dishes, cleaning, laundry, etc.

- The husband can leverage his understanding of his wife's strengths to be her career mentor.

- The dispensation of a wife claiming very personal ownership of her earnings is quickly fading away.

- As finance is a major area of marital conflict, couples should be transparent about their values around money right from courtship. This is also the ideal stage to decide if they will operate a joint account or not.

- The couple should quickly learn the marriage-strengthening language of joint asset ownership – "it's our money" – very early on in their marriage. The language "it is mine" is not very helpful in building an enduring marriage.

- Whatever their decision about money might be, the couple must work hard to ensure that money is only a blessing and not a curse that will wreck their marriage.

CHAPTER FOURTEEN

CARE, PROVISION, AND PROTECTION

If you love somebody, you care about that person. You'll often naturally extend that same care to anything that is important to them. Likewise, if you care about someone, you will also provide for and protect them, thus making caring, provision, and protection a cyclical process.

This cyclical process consists of mutual responsibilities that both the husband and the wife must share between them. The husband must deeply care for his wife by being sensitive to her needs. Those needs may be spiritual, emotional, financial, material, psychological, and so on. To identify her various needs, the husband would need to be sensitive and a keen observer. If the husband can proactively detect a need in his wife's life and make efforts to meet that need without being instructed, he will be doing well.

The husband must provide a home for his wife because safety and security are some of the most important needs of any woman. The need to feel safe and secure can come in the form of a home and finances to take care of expected or unforeseen exigencies. These requirements are necessary for her to relax, feel safe, be stable, and feel comfortable.

AREAS OF MUTUAL RESPONSIBILITY

In terms of protection, the husband must endeavor to protect his wife from physical, spiritual, emotional, or psychological attacks.

Physical protection

The mere presence of the husband should deter any type of aggression toward his wife. However, if the aggressor is daring enough to still try it, the husband must intervene promptly to protect his wife. Even before picking up the phone to dial 9-1-1, you must be prepared to provide this protection. According to Ephesians five, don't forget that you may literally have to give up your life, protecting your wife if it comes to that (Ephesians 5:25).

Protection from psychological attacks

Aside from physical protection, the husband may have to protect his wife against hostile family members who may attempt to torture or abuse her psychologically. You will have to stand up to such people and let them know that you will not tolerate this kind of behavior from anyone. To ensure that the message is clearly communicated, understood, and received, you must be firm about it.

Wife's care for her husband

The wife also has key care responsibilities toward her husband. Chief among such responsibilities is his well-being. And because every marriage is different, each case would involve understanding your husband's unique needs. For example, if you're a stay-at-home wife, one of your primary care responsibilities towards

AREAS OF MUTUAL RESPONSIBILITY

ensuring your husband's well-being would be to ensure that his nutritional needs are always met.

Very recently, I was in a discussion with my massage therapist, and she told me how she and her husband share duties at home. She was very emphatic that she loved her kitchen, to the point that she did not want her husband in there for cooking. However, according to her, she has reserved doing dishes and cleaning for him.

She added that her husband knows that if he wants to eat the next meal, there must not be any dirty dishes in the sink. I think that's very true for many couples. The wife whole-heartedly accepts the responsibility of cooking delicious meals for her husband and the children. And in many instances, she expects them to help with the dishes.

The wife's protective responsibility

God's primary justification for making a wife for Adam was that it was not good for the man to be alone. Therefore, God said that he would make for man a helper. Actually, the root word in Hebrew for "helper" is *ezer*, which means "to surround for the purpose of providing protection." That means that when God conceived the idea of making a wife for Adam, he had Eve's responsibility to protect her husband right at the core of that idea. Therefore, this understanding debunks the notion that only the husband should protect his wife.

Of course, it is common knowledge that the husband's duty is to protect his wife. It's a responsibility that I personally take very seriously. However, a thorough understanding of this word, on the other hand, suggests that protection is a mutual responsibility between the husband and his wife. As I spent time trying to understand why God would say that a woman would protect her husband, it became clear to me how this could be done. Let's have a look at some examples.

Very often, men drive themselves so hard towards success that they fail to remember to look after themselves properly. At such times, it will be the responsibility of a discerning wife to find ways to slow him down a bit so that he doesn't suffer burnout. Burnout is a horrible thing, and men are notorious for not being sensitive to it and all its devastating aftermaths. Who will argue that it is not an essential area of protection?

Another example is in the area of physical health. It is a fact that some men go on for years without periodic physical exams. Perhaps some of such men live in denial that, as men, they are too strong to need routine medical exams. They live in an unreal or non-existent world of being too strong to fall sick.

Meanwhile, it is true that early detection is the best way to handle many of the life-altering illnesses that we all are aware of. A caring and protective wife will notice this and, in some instances, will call the doctor's office to schedule an appointment for her husband's annual physical examination. Some women may even volunteer to accompany them to such appointments to encourage their husbands even more.

A protective wife can also protect her unsuspecting husband from seductive and ethically bankrupt women. Of course, some men who engage in unethical moral behavior such as infidelity do it intentionally and for various reasons. However, every wife must take her responsibility as her husband's protector in this area very seriously. They will be able to detect and establish a protective hedge around their husbands. After all, a man's wife is supposed to be his best and closest friend.

Sadly, not all couples have developed that expected level of closeness. In fact, some couples strangely find it awkward being seen to be close to each other outside the home. Let me emphasize that it is important for every couple to develop the mindset of being close to each other once they are engaged or as soon as they wed. If they are intentional and strategic about it, they will naturally come to be known as each other's closest friends. That way, no one will misconstrue their closeness as a manifestation of mistrust or suspicion on the wife's part, nor will it be awkward for the husband or observers.

> *A protective wife can also protect her unsuspecting husband from seductive and morally bankrupt women.*

KEY TAKE AWAY

- The husband must see to it that his wife feels safe and secure, as these are some of the inherent needs of any woman.

- A caring and God-fearing husband senses his wife's needs and proactively takes steps to meet those needs without being told.

- All-round protection of the wife remains one of the husband's most important responsibilities.

- A protective wife can help her husband pay close attention to his health.

- A good wife can protect her husband from morally bankrupt women.

CHAPTER FIFTEEN

PARTNERSHIP

A partnership is an arrangement where the concerned parties agree to cooperate to advance their mutual interests. Given our understanding, as I have described in the preceding pages, marriage is arguably the most important partnership there is. Even in ordinary circumstances, the two defining phrases that make up the word "partnership" are "agreement to cooperate" and "advance their mutual interests."

When it comes to a marriage partnership, the interests are no longer just mutual but joint or collective since the husband and his wife have become one flesh. The husband doesn't have interests different from his wife's, and vice versa. What were hitherto their individual interests have now merged into a well-packaged bundle of interests that both of them should share. Therefore, there should be no attempt to demarcate the wife's and husband's interests.

Patrick and Alexia's story

Not many years ago, my wife and I had the privilege of assisting a young couple in navigating what they saw as their individual interests. Patrick wanted to travel to Australia to pursue further professional qualifications. He wanted this so badly that he

AREAS OF MUTUAL RESPONSIBILITY

was determined to plow through with no consideration for the impact of his decision on his wife. He commanded Alexia, "If you are still interested in this marriage, you will have to quit your job so that we can travel together." This was going to be an open-ended undertaking. They didn't know when the training would start or end. On the other hand, Alexia was not very keen on leaving her regulated profession behind, only to come back and lose her license to practice.

We encouraged Patrick to think about Alexia's professional interests and how his plan would generally affect their marriage and their finances. Better ideas arose as soon as they looked at their common interests together. Patrick's desire to travel was shelved in favor of taking advantage of the opportunities available in Canada, which they both agreed on. He took a bit longer to complete the training he wanted locally, but he completed it successfully, and their marriage remained intact.

Marriage is an institution where team spirit reigns. As a team, there should be absolutely no competition or rivalry between the couple. You most probably have witnessed the terrible embarrassment of a team scoring against themselves in a sporting event. It usually makes news headlines the next day if it happens in a professional sport because no one expects something like this to happen.

> The husband doesn't have his own interests that are different from his wife's, and vice versa.

In most cases, a team works together to defeat an opponent. That's why a team that appears to oppose itself effectively turns

AREAS OF MUTUAL RESPONSIBILITY

into the general ridicule of the spectators. The inherent nature of what team play is supposed to be is negated in such a setting.

Teamwork should be a guiding principle in any high-functioning marriage. The husband and wife should always work collaboratively and as hard as possible to be a winning team. Therefore, there is no need for the spouses to conduct themselves as if they were competing against each other. That should never happen in a good and thriving marriage!

As is true of all team sports, the husband and his wife should always be seen as working together towards a common goal at any given point. It would be awesome to have them support each other to achieve their family goals together. They should also know that in marriage, it is either both are successful or both are losers. No spouse can win or lose alone. When one wins, it is a victory for both. So it is when one of them loses. That is part of the mystery of the husband and his wife becoming one flesh.

Kirk and Jacquie's story

Kirk and Jacquie were in the tenth year of their marriage when we met them. As it's fairly common with many people who move to a new country, they were still struggling to find their bearings. Expectedly, that struggle comes with multi-layered pressures. On one of the occasions during their frequent squabbles, Jacquie told Kirk, "I have wasted too much of my time with you in the name of marriage. You keep dragging me backward. I know where I would've been by now. I know the dreams I had for myself as a young woman. I am not meant to be a loser, but my association with you in the name of marriage, unfortunately, is making me one. And I can't continue this way."

AREAS OF MUTUAL RESPONSIBILITY

Such disparaging and condescending language doesn't belong in a Christian marriage because it can inflict irreparable damage to the image of your spouse and, ultimately, to your marriage itself. And indeed, Jacquie's words hurt Kirk so much that he walked out of the marriage. By the time we got involved, it was all too late. Kirk stood his ground that he wouldn't stand on Jacquie's path to greatness again. Never! he insisted.

My wife and I joined Jacquie to plead, but apparently, the psychological hurt was too deep for our plea to make a difference, as Kirk wouldn't listen. His position was that since his wife had told him that their marriage was making her a loser, then he was happy to move on so that Jacquie could achieve all her lofty childhood dreams.

> They should also know that in marriage, it is either both are successful, or both are losers. No couple can win or lose alone.

Regrettably, sometimes you hear a couple say very despicable things about each other as if they are no longer a team but rather two separate individuals.

I heard a wife ask her husband: "What exactly are you good at?" She went further to say, "…since we got married, I have carefully tried to identify what your real strength is. I still can't figure it out. Please, help me."

She continued, "Come to think of it, how many jobs have you lost?" She agonizingly concluded, "I am completely exhausted of the whole thing."

AREAS OF MUTUAL RESPONSIBILITY

I used this moment to remind her that she effectively referred to herself when she used such crude language toward her husband because she and her husband were one and not two different people. For the health of their marriage, couples must endeavor to understand the true meaning of becoming "one flesh."

A wise woman would use her energy and intellect to guarantee that the partnership she has formed with her husband is an exemplary one that works and ultimately honors God in every manner, rather than badmouthing and criticizing him.

> For the health of their marriage, couples must endeavor to understand the true meaning of becoming 'one flesh'.

It has been suggested that women tend to have more common sense than men, which they should use for the good of their marriage partnership. They have a unique perspective that many men don't appear to have. As a result, if a wife can leverage her ability to perceive what her husband can't see and communicate it to him effectively, she will become an indispensable asset to her husband. I believe this to be another good reason why the Bible says that he who finds a wife finds a good thing and steps into a place of favor with God. (Proverbs 18:22)

Teamwork in the biblical story of Abigail

Every man would treasure a wife in the caliber of biblical Abigail, originally Nabal's wife, who used her excellent qualities to engrave her name in gold. In fact, the Bible describes her as intelligent and beautiful in appearance, and her personality was true to that description.

AREAS OF MUTUAL RESPONSIBILITY

Here is part of this captivating account recorded in First Samuel 25:2-13 (New American Standard Bible).

> *Now there was a man in Maon whose business was in Carmel; and the man was very rich, and he had three thousand sheep and a thousand goats. And it came about while he was shearing his sheep in Carmel (now the man's name was Nabal, and his wife's name was Abigail. And the woman was intelligent and beautiful in appearance, but the man was harsh and evil in his dealings, and he was a Calebite), that David heard in the wilderness that Nabal was shearing his sheep.*
>
> *So David sent ten young men; and David said to the young men, "Go up to Carmel, visit Nabal and greet him in my name; and thus you shall say, "Have a long life, peace be to you, and peace be to your house, and peace be to all that you have. Now I have heard that you have shearers; now your shepherds have been with us, and we have not insulted them, nor have they missed anything all the days they were in Carmel.*
>
> *Ask your young men, and they will tell you. Therefore, let my young men find favor in your eyes, for we have come on a festive day. Please give whatever you find at hand to your servants and to your son David.'" When David's young men came, they spoke to Nabal according to all these words in David's name; then they waited.*

AREAS OF MUTUAL RESPONSIBILITY

> *But Nabal answered David's servants and said, "Who is David? And who is the son of Jesse? There are many servants today who are each breaking away from his master. Shall I then take my bread and my water and my meat that I have slaughtered for my shearers and give it to men whose origin I do not know?" So David's young men retraced their way and went back; and they came and told him according to all these words.*
>
> *David said to his men, "Each of you gird on his sword." So each man girded on his sword. And David also girded on his sword, and about four hundred men went up behind David while two hundred stayed with the baggage.*

Now, one of Nabal's servants actually corroborated David's narrative in Verse 8 above. The young man further suggested to Abigail to consider what she could do in a timely manner; otherwise, evil was imminently coming against Nabal and his whole household.

Here is what Abigail quickly did: "*Then Abigail hurried and took two hundred loaves of bread and two jugs of wine and five sheep already prepared and five measures of roasted grain and a hundred clusters of raisins and two hundred cakes of figs, and loaded them on donkeys. She said to her young men, 'Go on before me; behold, I am coming after you.' But she did not tell her husband Nabal.*" 1 Samuel 25:18-19

The example of Abigail's efforts in teamwork can best be described in the following characteristics.

AREAS OF MUTUAL RESPONSIBILITY

Common Sense and good judgement

First, Abigail had a rare sound judgment, which made her quickly perceive the magnitude of what was at stake. She knew that her timely intervention was required to prevent the pogrom that was about to take place. She also used her rare sense of judgment to assign the appropriate level of priority. Consequently, she left the party that she and her husband were hosting to urgently attend to what deserved her attention the most.

Humble and Gracious

Second, Abigail was a humble woman with an excellent gift of discernment who knew how to use gracious words to entreat and soften the heart of an unstoppable warrior like David, who was coming against her family. Her gracious words delivered the same outcome that King Solomon said that were a honeycomb, sweet to the soul and healing to the bones.

Here is her excellent and gracious intercession before David:

> When Abigail saw David, she hurried and dismounted from her donkey, and fell on her face before David and bowed herself to the ground. She fell at his feet and said,
>
> *"On me alone, my lord, be the blame. And please let your maidservant speak to you and listen to the words of your maidservant. Please do not let my lord pay attention to this worthless man, Nabal, for as his name is, so is he. Nabal is his name and folly is with him; but I your maidservant did not see the young men of my lord whom you sent.*

AREAS OF MUTUAL RESPONSIBILITY

"Now therefore, my lord, as the Lord lives, and as your soul lives, since the Lord has restrained you from shedding blood, and from avenging yourself by your own hand, now then let your enemies and those who seek evil against my lord, be as Nabal. Now let this gift which your maidservant has brought to my lord be given to the young men who accompany my lord.

"Please forgive the transgression of your maidservant; for the Lord will certainly make for my lord an enduring house, because my lord is fighting the battles of the Lord, and evil will not be found in you all your days.

Should anyone rise up to pursue you and to seek your life, then the life of my lord shall be bound in the bundle of the living with the Lord your God; but the lives of your enemies He will sling out as from the hollow of a sling.

And when the Lord does for my lord according to all the good that He has spoken concerning you, and appoints you ruler over Israel, this will not cause grief or a troubled heart to my lord, both by having shed blood without cause and by my lord having avenged himself. When the Lord deals well with my lord, then remember your maidservant" (1 Samuel 25:23-31).

AREAS OF MUTUAL RESPONSIBILITY

A gentle and sweet spirit

Thirdly, Abigail was of a gentle and sweet spirit, respectful of her husband. Verse 36 says that Abigail came to Nabal, and behold, he was holding a feast in his house, like the feast of a king. And Nabal's heart was merry within him, for he was very drunk, so she did not tell him anything at all until the morning light.

She didn't bother to make any noise or create a scene in front of all the guests at the party. She allowed the party to go on as if nothing of that magnitude nearly happened. She disclosed it to her husband only the following day.

Wise Restrainer

Fourth and arguably most importantly, she saved David from being guilty of mass murder. When David sat back and reflected on all that had just happened, he was deeply grateful for the wisdom that Abigail had displayed. He undoubtedly knew that, but for Abigail's wise and timely intervention, he would have committed appalling acts of mass murder, which would have undoubtedly haunted him throughout his life. No wonder the Bible says that wisdom is the principal thing; therefore, get wisdom. And in all your getting, get wisdom. (Proverbs 4:7)

Reward for her rare attributes

Then David said to Abigail, "Blessed be the Lord God of Israel, who sent you this day to meet me, and blessed be your discernment, and blessed be you, who have kept me this day from bloodshed and from avenging myself by my own hand.

AREAS OF MUTUAL RESPONSIBILITY

Nevertheless, as the Lord God of Israel lives, who has restrained me from harming you, unless you had come quickly to meet me, surely there would not have been left to Nabal until the morning light as much as one male."

So David received from her hand what she had brought him and said to her, "Go up to your house in peace. See, I have listened to you and granted your request."

Abigail's overall personality can only be described as quintessential and a classic for us all, particularly for wives to emulate. King David knew immediately that as king, he needed Abigail for a wife such that immediately following Nabal's death, David proposed to Abigail and proceeded to marry her. And even today, women with such qualities will make their husbands great men who will earn a place of honor in society.

That's the kind of teamwork and influence that accomplishes great results. Those are the type of results that position the husband and the whole family on the trajectory of good success. That's the kind of initiative in which a wise woman should channel her energy. That will be a much better use of her positive energy and intellect. The wife's effort to control the husband will be ill-advised, wasteful, and a misdirected effort because that is not her role in a marriage.

Note that, as is the case with most humans, Abigail is by no means a perfect individual. For instance, other commentators have suggested that she went slightly too far in some of her utterances against her husband, Nabal, in her attempt to pacify David. However, it should be noted that I have solely focused on the positive aspects of her life in presenting the lessons that we can all learn from. Maybe her attributes which some may see as negative, will be the subject of a future book.

KEY TAKE AWAY

- As Paul tells us in Ephesians 5:32, marriage is a unique partnership.

- Marriage is a partnership like no other.

- Marriage is a partnership where the victory of one spouse means victory for both. Similarly, one spouse's loss is inevitably a loss for the couple.

- The mystery of being "one flesh" in marriage means that hauling disparaging remarks at your spouse invariably means self-disparagement.

- In marriage, each spouse's strength should be celebrated to complement his or her spouse to make the partnership complete.

CHAPTER SIXTEEN

SEXUAL INTIMACY

"If a man or a woman fails to thank God for the gift of sex, they will not thank Him for anything else." – Pastor Frantz Lamour, Holy Church of Grace, West Palm Beach, Fl. USA.

"Sex between a husband and a wife is never a cause for shame. It should be honoured, cherished and enjoyed as the gift and the good that it is; thanks be to God!" – Pastor Paul Carter, Cornerstone Baptist Church, Orillia, Ontario. Canada.

Who is sexual intimacy for?

It is important for me to state upfront that God's original concept of sexual intimacy was intended for married people—husband and wife. Therefore, as exciting as this chapter and the benefits of sex outlined below may sound, if you are single reading this book, I will strongly advise you to wait until you are married because God's beautiful idea regarding sex was created to be enjoyed only in the context of marriage.

It should be carefully noted that sex outside marriage is fornication, and it is not recommended! Paul said this to the Corinthians: "Nevertheless, because of sexual immorality, let each man have his own wife, and let each woman have her own husband" (1 Corinthians 7:2). This advice includes all other forms of sexual expressions, such as petting and masturbation.

People who are engaged to be married should exercise self-control, be patient and wait until they are married. You don't want to engage in something that will make you feel guilty or regretful later in life.

Pastor Tim Keller once said, *"Sex within marriage is a powerful statement of exclusive commitment and faithfulness to the other person."*

As any married person can attest, when sex is enjoyed in an atmosphere of such exclusive commitment and faithfulness to one another in a marital setting, there is usually a great deal of emotional satisfaction and happiness. On the other hand, such emotional satisfaction or happiness is hardly achieved when sexual intimacy occurs outside of marriage.

Therefore, it is impossible to overstate the fact that sex is one of the most beautiful ideas that God has created and handed over to humanity as a gift to enjoy. Right after they were created, Adam and Eve engaged in sex freely, without inhibition of any kind. In Genesis 2, we learn that Adam and Eve were both naked but were not ashamed at all.

Imagine that scene for a moment where a covering of any kind was not known to be part of the first couple. They unashamedly had no clothes on at any given moment. It is probably safe to assume that perhaps they were set for sexual activity as freely and consistently as possible. In his wisdom, God created sex to be enjoyed by the couple as husband and wife. As Adam and

Eve were back then in the Garden of Eden, there absolutely should be no shame about sexual intimacy between married couples today.

What is the purpose of Sex?

Sex has two main purposes. The first is for enjoyment, as I've stated above. The second purpose is for procreation. God commanded Adam and Eve to procreate and fill the earth. Interestingly, for most couples, this second purpose follows the first without necessarily being intentional about it. In other words, children come simply as a result of enjoying sex. That's truly beautiful indeed!

Sex in our contemporary world

Perhaps only a few people will disagree that the world has hijacked sex and is trying everything under the sun to distort and devalue it. For instance, in some countries of the developed world, a legislated framework exists that recognizes sex as a trade. In such countries, sex has been placed on par with the well-known traditional trades such as plumbing or carpentry. Those who are engaged in it are often referred to as being in sex trade or sex workers. As a result, prostitution has been legalized in such jurisdictions, and women who sell sex must pay taxes in the same way that other workers do. Isn't that odd and heart-wrenching?

With that level of depravity, I would like to assert that it is no longer acceptable for the church to merely say that the world should be left alone to continue distorting one of God's most precious gift to humanity. Without a doubt, the church must intervene so that we can reclaim sex and reveal its true beauty, as well as the reason why God created it in the first place. However, to achieve that, I believe that the church needs to emphasize sex education more than it is currently doing.

> *For instance, in some parts of the developed world, sex is now regarded as a trade, and placed on par with trades such as plumbing or carpentry.*

I feel a sense of urgency to emphasize this because, sadly, some people get uncomfortable or even cringe when sex is mentioned from the pulpit or in other Christian settings. That shouldn't be the case! If those who understand what sex represents talk about it the way they should, there is an assurance that they will do so appropriately and with the right motive. It will be akin to hearing it from the right source.

Arguably, the church has come a long way in this regard, however, I am confident that increased emphasis will help to straighten some of the skewed understanding of the subject of sex from many church-going people. Think about it for a moment, if sex were a bad thing or something to be ashamed of, God wouldn't have created it in the first place because as James 1:17 tells us, every good gift and every perfect gift comes from the Lord. In other words, it is created by God and it's good and even perfect.

> *If sex were a bad thing or something to be ashamed of, God would not have created it...*

AREAS OF MUTUAL RESPONSIBILITY

The role of parents in sex education

Parents have an important role to play in ensuring that their children receive solid, age-appropriate sex education. It may be an uncomfortable reality for some parents to discover that in many jurisdictions children are already learning about sex as part of their school curriculum. They are also learning about it from some of their friends on the playground and in fact, elsewhere.

I am not ignorant that there is a division within the Christian community on this issue. I am aware that some parents do not support sex education of any kind for their children. I know it because I was born and raised in such a family background. However, I think those were morally much safer days than today. Given the apparent moral perversion in our world today, I will advocate that parents should be the primary source of such an essential area of education for their children. As an integral part of that education, parents must also create an open and honest channel of communication with their children, whereby their children can feel comfortable enough to approach them with any questions that they may have about sex.

Let it be known that if parents fail to effectively play that role of educating their children about sex in a timely manner, their children will, regrettably, learn it from an untrusted source. Sadly, those are sources that could harm your children. By the way, did you know that *one in four girls and one in six boys will be sexually abused before they turn 18 years old? (Source: www.ywca.org)*. As a result, parents must strive to stay ahead of the curve, especially in this information age, where nothing is undercover anymore. This website, www.teachingsexualhealth.ca, contains useful information that some parents may find helpful as they

AREAS OF MUTUAL RESPONSIBILITY

seek ways to provide age-appropriate sex education for their children.

> *If those who understand what sex represents talk about it the way they should, there is an assurance that they will communicate it appropriately and with the right motive.*

What the Bible says about sex

Paul penned these revolutionary words in his first letter to the Corinthians:

> "Now concerning the things of which you wrote to me: It is good for a man not to touch a woman. Nevertheless, because of sexual immorality, let each man have his own wife, and let each woman have her own husband. Let the husband render to his wife the affection due her, and likewise also the wife to her husband. The wife does not have authority over her own body, but the husband does. And likewise, the husband does not have authority over his own body, but the wife does. <u>Do not deprive one another except with consent for a time, that you may give yourselves to fasting and prayer; and come together again so that Satan does not tempt you because of your lack of self-control</u>" (1 Corinthians 7:1–5 The underlines are mine for discussion below).

AREAS OF MUTUAL RESPONSIBILITY

Spouses owe each other sexual pleasure and satisfaction

Roy E. Ciampa and Brian S. Rosner have provided the following important commentary about the above scripture:

"The marked mutuality of Paul's comments (the husband has authority over his wife's body and she has authority over his) was, however, revolutionary in the ancient world where patriarchy was the norm. For the husband to have authority over his wife's body was nothing special.... Paul's following statement affirming the reverse, that "the husband does not have authority over his own body, but the wife does," clearly pointed to a radical and unprecedented restriction on the husbands' sexual freedom. It communicates, negatively, his obligation to refrain from engaging in sexual relations with anyone other than his wife and, positively, his obligation to fulfill his marital duty to provide her with sexual pleasure and satisfaction."[13]

The idea that sex was to be mutual and that the husband owed it to his wife – and that the wife had a right to claim it from her husband – was revolutionary! In fact, it was unprecedented! According to Roy and Brian, no one had ever said anything like this anywhere else in the first-century world.

Far from parroting the sexual norms of the culture, Christianity taught that sex within a marriage should be free, generous, and reciprocal. That counsel was at odds with the norms of the first-century Roman Empire, and to a large extent, it remains at odds with the wisdom of our secular culture today.

For example, there are still some in the church today who believe that couples should only have sex when both parties desire it.

AREAS OF MUTUAL RESPONSIBILITY

Those who seek to advance such a doctrine always claim that a spouse's demand for sexual intimacy is selfish if the other spouse does not desire it. That notion flies in the face of Paul's counsel, which clearly says that sex should be given in marriage whenever either party desires it. Of all the things said in the Bible about sex, I think this could be one of the most surprising of them all. It truly is a paradigm shift! However, couples must avoid marital rape which is not allowed in many parts of the developed world. No spouse should force his or her way on their spouse.

> But couples must avoid marital rape, which is a crime in most of the developed world.

1 Corinthians 5:1-5 above unambiguously states that neither the husband nor the wife should make their partner feel that they are being a bother when it comes to the issue of sex. I am not ignorant that it is not unusual for one partner not to be immediately in the mood or ready for sex at a particular time, but this scripture clearly mandates both couples to lovingly respond to each other by taking steps "to be ready." Often, this requires some patience from both couples.

Married couples should have it often

As we saw above, Paul told the Corinthians this: Do not deprive one another except with consent for a time, that you may give yourselves to fasting and prayer; and come together again so that Satan does not tempt you because of your lack of self-control.

Although Paul's instruction about when couples may consider abstaining from sexual intimacy seems straightforward, it appears to have been misunderstood by more than a few these days. I am somewhat suspicious that perhaps, that misunderstanding may be intentional for some people. And I hope I am not wrong about this. I have underlined three parts of the above scripture that often require further clarification for many.

The ills of using sex as bargaining chip

Sadly, some wives withhold sex from their husbands when they want him to do or give them something. Their behavior clearly suggests something like this: "if you want sex, let me have what I have asked you to give me". Such a behavior is inappropriate. That behavior doesn't belong in a Christian marriage. It is only those sell sex that oblige their clients only if the agreed price has been paid.

Igor and Wanda's story

During one of my marriage enrichment event a few years ago, a participant shared the following hilarious story about certain middle aged couple he nicknamed Igor and Wanda. Wanda had starved her husband of sex over an extended period of time because she wanted Igor to buy her a new car. This went on for such a long time that Igor became very frustrated with his wife. This fateful morning, Wanda had set up table for breakfast which included honey for oat she had prepared. She invited her husband to the dinning table. On getting to the table, Igor grabbed the bottle of honey, walked over to the sink and emptied the honey down the sink. He went even further to thoroughly rinse the bottle and then threw it in the recycling bin.

Wanda was just starring at him as he was carrying out the drama. Then she asked her husband, "what's the meaning of

AREAS OF MUTUAL RESPONSIBILITY

this that you have just done?" He responded, "well, you have resolved that nobody will enjoy something sweet in this house, so you too will not drink oat with honey."

No couple should allow this kind of drama to occur in their marriage. It is not necessary and should be avoided.

The Bible saying that married couples could set aside some days for dedicated prayer and spiritual observance—only if both parties agree—but then they must come together quickly lest they be tempted to do something they're not supposed to do—that is, fall into sexual temptation.

As in the Old Testament and the New Testament, frequent sexual intimacy between married couples is biblically prescribed as a guard against a wandering eye and a lustful heart. According to Proverbs 5:15, the assumption is that if we drink deeply from our own cisterns, we'll not be tempted to draw from our neighbor's well. There is great wisdom and joy in following this important instruction.

The first part of first Corinthians 7:5 states the condition when abstinence may be required. Paul said, *"... except with consent."* This means that couples need to seek and obtain consent from each other not to engage in sexual activity for a limited time. The simple meaning of consent is to obtain permission for something to happen or an agreement to do something.

The whole point of first seeking and obtaining permission to fast and pray is that it is quite possible the other spouse may deny that permission. For instance, if your teenage child asks you for permission to go and visit a friend and you say no, you will expect them not to go. In such situations, a parent

AREAS OF MUTUAL RESPONSIBILITY

will normally say something like this "But you don't have my consent to go where you want to." If they insist and go, you will consider them ill-mannered and disobedient.

It's similar to a husband asking his wife for permission to fast and pray while they both abstain from sexual activity. The wife has the right to refuse. Of course, that's the whole point of consent. There should be an expectation that it could be declined. Although one may be disappointed, there's nothing wrong about saying no in such a situation.

A wife who elects to decline her husband's request for consent may say something like this: "Honey, I have been looking forward to us having great sex, and I cannot join you in the prayer and fast program that you want us to have." Or she may say, "Perhaps, if you want us to go on the prayer and fasting together, then let us move it to next week, but let us have a good time in bed over the next couple of days first." Alternatively, she may suggest, "You can go ahead and fast and pray all you want, but I need us to make love at this time."

A wife who makes any of the above suggestions should not be considered a pervert or unspiritual. She is not! Neither should such suggestions be viewed as an abomination. One spouse asks for consent to abstain from sex, and the other either outrightly declines or suggests some alternatives. I believe that was the message Paul was communicating to the Corinthians.

I caution Christians to be careful and not attempt to create an impression that their moral standards and level of spirituality are higher than those of God himself. Doing so will give you away as hypocritical. None of us will ever have a higher moral standard close to that of our Heavenly Father. Never?

AREAS OF MUTUAL RESPONSIBILITY

After all, if there is a need to fast and pray, the first person who will know is your spouse. Therefore, unless your motive is to deny your spouse sex, you shouldn't be asking for time off to fast and pray when your spouse doesn't even know what the urgent need really is.

Paul also states the duration. He said, *"... for a time."* That simply means the consent not to have sexual intimacy should be for a limited time. It should not be for an extended period. He also provided why this duration should not be long or open-ended – so that Satan may not take advantage of the supposedly glorious time with God to tempt you.

Geoff and Shannon's story.

A couple of years ago, I learned of an interesting situation in a church where the senior pastor declared that the whole church should fast and pray for forty days. The unannounced expectation was that couples would not have sexual intimacy while the fasting period lasted. Two weeks into the program, some of the men could no longer handle it. They started making sexual advances toward their wives.

As a result, some of the women individually came and reported their husbands to their pastor. One of the women, Shannon, approached their pastor and asked for clarification.

She started this way: "Reverend, I have a problem."

Their Reverend asked her, "What's the problem?"

She went on, "Are we supposed to be having sex during this period that we are fasting or not?"

AREAS OF MUTUAL RESPONSIBILITY

The Reverend replied, "It is better to abstain from sex throughout these forty days. Why did you ask?"

Shannon responded, "I thought so, but I think you will need to talk to Geoff. I don't know what is wrong with him. He is not spiritual at all. We are only two weeks into this program, and every night after breaking the fast, he will be frantically making advances for sexual intimacy."

This is precisely the kind of thing that Paul was warning the Corinthians about. Some people may find it easy to blame those men. But the fact that they are fasting does not change the very human nature regarding the desire for sex. It is quite possible that most of the men and women in that church may have been able to go through the forty days with enough self-control and not have sex. But it should not be assumed that every married couple should be able to exercise that level of self-control. Unless, perhaps, we are suggesting that Paul was wrong or unspiritual himself.

Benefits of sex

For some couples, the real desire for sex is mainly about having babies. Then there is another section of the population whose interest in sex is simply about the great feeling you get when you do it. However, several studies have shown that there are some real health benefits for both men and women that may come as a pleasant surprise to some people. The benefits of sex are more than procreation and enjoyment.

"Having sex regularly can do more than make you feel closer to your partner—it can actually make you physically healthier." - Hilda Hutcherson, M.D.

AREAS OF MUTUAL RESPONSIBILITY

"Twisting the sheets comes with a slew of body-boosting side effects."
- Cari Wira Dineen.

Benefits of sex for men

- Sex can lower your chance of prostate cancer.
- A great sexual activity means a sweet night's rest. Sex is well known as a very effective sleeping pill.
- Sex will make you fit and potentially live longer – sex is a very good cardio and general physical exercise. And we know that physical exercise is essential for healthy living, and healthy living can lead to an extended life expectancy.

Sex benefits for women

Studies have shown that women who indulge in sex will stand to experience the following benefits:

- Fewer colds
- A youthful glow
- A more toned bod

KEY TAKE-AWAYS

- For a Christian, sex is reserved for married people only. Sex outside of marriage is a sin and is strongly discouraged.

- Sex between a husband and his wife is a powerful statement of exclusive commitment and faithfulness to each other.

- Sex between a husband and his wife should be enjoyed, honored, and cherished as a precious gift from God.

- It is no longer acceptable for the Church to simply turn its face away and allow the ungodly world to continue with the distortion of sex, God's precious gift to mankind.

- Together with the Church, Christian parents, need to actively engage in age-appropriate sex education to help children inculcate a biblical understanding of sex and what it is all about.

- Paul commands that couples should not deprive each other of sexual intimacy, <u>except with consent and for a limited time</u>.

- It doesn't necessarily mean that there must be abstinence from sex during prayer and fasting.

- Regular sexual activity comes with many great health benefits for men which include:

    o   Sex can lower your chance of prostate cancer

    o   Get a good night of rest.

    o   Regular sexual intimacy can contribute to your physical fitness and consequently live longer

- Health benefits of regular sex for women include:

    o   Fewer colds

    o   A youthful glow

    o   A more toned bod

CHAPTER SEVENTEEN

BEQUEATHING LEGACIES

For couples who have children, bequeathing legacies will be an important area of mutual responsibility that they will have to take seriously. In fact, it is nearly impossible to articulate sufficiently the significance of this area of joint responsibility between the husband and his wife. Family legacies can be worth treasuring and passing on to the next generation. They're important because being aware of your family legacy can help you decide which beliefs and attitudes you cherish and which you want to make a conscious effort to change. Quite clearly, this chapter doesn't apply to couples who, for one reason or another, do not have children.

Most married people will agree that once children start arriving in a marriage, a greater sense of responsibility automatically comes upon the parents. Though an unwritten code of conduct, the coming of children in marriage also comes with an impartation of a sense of maturity, or at least, so it should.

While there are many legacies that a couple can bequeath to their children, we will discuss two legacies that I consider to be the minimum and most essential that any Christian couple should strive to leave for their children.

AREAS OF MUTUAL RESPONSIBILITY

The two legacies are:

- A life of faith.
- A lifetime of marital bliss.

A legacy of a life of faith

This is arguably the most important legacy any Christian parent can leave for their children. This is because a life of faith transcends everything else that really matters in this earthly life. A life built on the foundation of faith will last for a lifetime and beyond. Evidence shows that when a life of faith is accorded the right priority, one's life stands a much better chance of getting other important aspects of life straight. I find that everything else that truly matters flows from one's life of faith. When we teach our children to seek first the kingdom of God and his righteousness, we are effectively teaching them to set a tone for a well-rounded, successful life. When we, with our households, can vigorously demonstrate that by placing our faith in God above all else, he will be gracious to add all the other things every human being tends to care so much about.

For this reason, the husband and the wife should work painstakingly as a team to create that solid foundation of faith in the home. The children need it as a foundation on which to build their lives. This thought process and advice are consistent with Jesus' teaching as recorded in Matthew 6:19-34.

In his second letter to Timothy, Paul wrote that in the last days, there would come times of difficulty. For people will be lovers of self, lovers of money, proud, arrogant, abusive, disobedient to their parents, ungrateful, unholy, heartless, unappeasable, slanderous, without self-control, brutal, not loving good, treacherous, reckless, swollen with conceit, lovers of pleasure rather than lovers of God, having the appearance of godliness, but denying its power. (2 Timothy 3:1-5)

I believe the days described in the above passage are arguably beginning to emerge right before our eyes. And their emergence is only going to continue to unfold with unrelenting intensity. We must not forget to build a connection between Paul's message above and Jesus' teaching in Matthew 24:13. Jesus said that because iniquity shall greatly increase during those days, there will be a corresponding diminishing love of many who will be alive at that time. If the Bible says it, take note, it will come to pass!

However, the life of faith is what is going to separate those who will thrive to the end and those who will become victims of those perilous days. It is important to note what Jesus added to his teaching in Matthew 24 that only those who will stand firm through those difficult times will be saved. And what a beautiful legacy it is for the children to grow up and say, "Glory be to God, our parents bequeathed a life of faith to us. Hence, we are able to thrive despite the very challenging times." That will be a priceless testimony and a towering legacy.

> And what a beautiful legacy it is for our children to grow up and say Glory be to God, our parents bequeathed a life of faith to us, hence we are able to thrive despite the very challenging times.

AREAS OF MUTUAL RESPONSIBILITY

How to raise children in an atmosphere of faith

It has been commonly said that no one can give what he or she doesn't have. That means that to raise children in an atmosphere of faith, the parents themselves must first be able and ready to live an observable life of faith. Children are well-known for their propensity to be good imitators of their mentors or any adult under whose sphere of influence they are growing up. In fact, children and most young people copy anything they see others do, good or bad. That is why parents are best suited to point their children in the right direction in all matters, including matters of faith.

Such propensity of children is so strong that it can best be described as children saying: "show me, don't tell me." In other words, typically, children will say, "If I see you do it, then I will follow suit and be your copycat." It is for this same reason that the onus should be on parents to be excellent role models for their children as people who live by faith and not by sight.

Dependence on God

As parents, one of the most important things we can show our children as we help them develop a life of faith is for us to demonstrate complete dependence on the Almighty God as our Father, who is our faithful provider, protector, enabler, and sustainer. This can be demonstrated through a consistent life of prayer. Naturally, children look up to their parents as their providers, protectors, enablers, and sustainers. In fact, they look up to their parents for virtually everything.

Therefore, when children observe that their parents are, in turn, genuinely dependent on somebody else, it communicates a very powerful message to them. The implication for young children is that "We thought that our dad and mom are capable of doing anything; they provide all the food and shelter for the family, they buy us clothes and shoes. Mom and dad are also physically big and strong. Therefore, this God that they are always praying to as their Heavenly Father must be really powerful, well above mom's and dad's ability."

As they continue to watch this consistent pattern of dependence on God, they start forming their own personal faith in this great and awesome Father that even mom and dad routinely turn to for help. This is what makes prayer one of the most effective ways to help children learn how to put their confidence in God instead of putting it in mom and dad or any other source. We should all remember what the Bible says in Proverbs 22:7. That scripture says that parents should train up their children the way they should go, so that when the children are old, they will not depart from it.

Prayer is very important. However, in our effort to help our children develop a life of faith, they must not merely see prayer as a means to go to God only when they are in need. It is critical that they comprehend this and regard prayer as a primary means of establishing intimacy with God. And in the process of that intimacy, God can meet their needs as the case may be.

The Word of God

Equally very important in our effort to help build a life of faith in children is for mom and dad to emphasize the authority of God's word—the Bible. Prayer and the Word must go together in this effort. And to do this effectively, the parents' knowledge of God's Word becomes very important. The Bible is important

AREAS OF MUTUAL RESPONSIBILITY

and helps us grow in our knowledge of who God is. And in the process of developing some depth in our knowledge of God, it also helps us build our faith.

Learning how to fall in love with God's Word happens simultaneously with falling in love with God himself. We learn how to become a Christian with a deep persuasion through God's Word. In other words, the Bible is the final authority that contains complete details of God's plan for salvation. Therefore, when we guide our children into developing a personal love for God and his Word, they understand and accept God's plan of salvation. When that happens, their faith is now built upon their personal conviction and not just their mom and dad's faith. And that's the foundation upon which we need to raise our children.

Commitment to the local church

Furthermore, in our efforts to help our children develop a life of faith, we must try to be an active part of a local church family. Being an active part of a church introduces them to an essential part of Christian living, which happens simultaneously with the growth of our faith. Besides, this is an important point as we increasingly see many Christians these days struggling to understand why they should be an active part of a local church and regularly attend worship services.

Such people fall into two categories: the first category is those who feel that it is good enough if they can attend a congregational worship service every once in a while. The second category is made up of people who have argued that they usually watch their favorite pastors on television or online. They conclude that doing so seems to be working just fine for them and their

AREAS OF MUTUAL RESPONSIBILITY

families. They also conclude that they don't need to attend in-person church services.

Although the space in this book will not be enough for me to exhaustively explain why it is important for you to be an active part of a church family, let me highlight the following key points: Proverbs 27:17 tells us that iron sharpens iron, and one man brightens the countenance of his friend. That means when we come together in person, we tend to positively impact one another in a way that would not be possible otherwise.

Of course, this isn't just the chance to sit in the same room as others. The atmosphere, even the limited interactions with others, might help take someone outside of themselves. Even when in-person meetings result in clashes due to personality differences, it's hard to dispute their relevance. When such personality differences are managed well, they tend to help us grow and mature in the long run.

Also, we need to understand that being an active part of a church family is not just about you alone. A very important part of that lifestyle gives you opportunities to help encourage or build other fellow believers. It's essential to understand that others need you, even if you personally feel you do not need them.

Unfortunately, with strictly online services, such opportunities become very limited or even non-existent. As you grow and mature, you'll find that the need for you to become a growth-enabling contributor to the kingdom of God becomes critical (Hebrews 5:11-14). In other words, as you mature as a Christian, you don't want to be seen simply as a receiver or consumer, but as you receive, you look for opportunities to make a positive impact on other members of your faith community. Therefore, limiting yourself only to online services will not give you many opportunities to enrich the lives of others spiritually. And it is essential to remember that you don't have to be a pastor to do this.

Finally, and most importantly, I will also point you to Hebrews 10:25, which strongly urges us not to neglect meeting together. I will recommend the local church where the Holy Spirit is recognized as the one in charge of everything, whom we absolutely cannot do without.

The above three activities have been proven to help children develop their faith as they watch as well as participate alongside their parents. As parents, we must always be aware that children learn by watching their parents or other role models live their lives. As a result, children who see their parents pray, study the Bible, and attend church regularly are more likely to adopt the same lifestyle when they become adults. This is analogous to reproducing your very best self out of your children.

Bequeath a lifetime of marital bliss

To put this point of bequeathing a lifetime of marital bliss into proper perspective, let me start this section with Aesop's fable about the goose and the golden egg.

> That fable goes like this:
>
> *There was a poor farmer who discovers that his goose is laying golden eggs. At first, the farmer thinks it must be a trick. But when he gets the eggs appraised, he learns they're actually pure gold!*

AREAS OF MUTUAL RESPONSIBILITY

The farmer still can't believe it. And he gets even more excited when he realizes the goose is laying golden eggs every day. Eventually, the farmer becomes fabulously wealthy.

But the farmer tires of caring for the goose and waiting day after day for the golden eggs. So he decides to kill the goose and get all the golden eggs at once. But when he opens the goose, there are no golden eggs. And now the goose is gone too.

Let's try and understand how this fable relates to marriage. A good marital relationship lays many golden eggs: security, companionship, sexual, intimacy, and so on. And that's precisely how we feel when we are in a high-functioning and thriving marriage. We feel whole and complete.

Experience has proven that, over time, we get so busy with our everyday cares, forget to pay attention to our partners, and don't have the time to do the things that facilitate falling in love with them as we should. In fact, most people become self-centered and impatient in how they relate to each other. The implication of such behavior is that the couples stop nurturing their marriage the way that it deserves.

As most people know, at the beginning of most marriages, the spousal relationship is quite strong with full of deep affection. However, if you want your spouse to keep laying the golden eggs, you must intentionally learn how to take care of them one day at a time without faltering.

When I was in my late teen years, I heard a marriage counselor say something that has stuck with me and has become part of

AREAS OF MUTUAL RESPONSIBILITY

my family and spiritual DNA. He said that one of the most important things a father can do for his children is to love their mom. Now that I'm married with children, I can explain why this is very important. First, as a husband and father, I know I've got to lead by example. So, if I am loving my wife, I am setting an example that love must always be at the center of everything in our home. Furthermore, as I've severally alluded to in this book, one of the leading need of every woman in a marriage is love.

Therefore, I know that if I am successful at providing my wife that love, she will feel secure and stable, making the home a happy place, which is important for the healthy growth of the children. Finally, when a father loves his wife, he's automatically giving his children the best gift at the same time. This explains why almost any child will tell you what an awful experience it is to watch their parents openly disagree, yell at each other or even fight.

I feel richly blessed to be able to attest to my parents' happy marriage. However, the few times I witnessed them disagree were some of the saddest moments of my life. Unfortunately, in some households, parents openly disagree and regularly fight in front of their children. That's terrible! Any young child can be psychologically traumatized by such a situation. If this pertains to you as a parent, please do everything you can to put a stop to it. Look for support if you need it to change.

A peaceful and healthy marriage is worth everything you have got. It is good for the parents, emotionally, physically, and even spiritually. It is even better for the children. It is good in every way. Therefore, don't spare any effort in ensuring that you attain it. A successful courtship and an elaborate wedding ceremony are only the beginning of a lifelong undertaking called marriage. You must work on your marriage as tirelessly as possible to make it an exemplary home for your children.

Here are some practical things you can do to achieve marital bliss:

Arrival of kids and the changing family dynamics

Nearly every couple looks forward to the arrival of children in their marriage. And it is an understatement to suggest that the arrival of children comes with unspeakable joy. However, a child's arrival sometimes tends to create a gap between the couple for various reasons, including post-partum depression for the mom. So, it's important for mom and dad to watch out to make sure that the children bring only additional joy between them and not distance.

In addition, parents should be proactive and talk ahead of time about raising their kids. They should discuss and make plans around things such as how best to support each other, not to disagree in front of the kids, or how to discipline them. These are some things that often influence the change in the family's dynamics with the arrival of kids. And it's important for parents to be able to pivot, change, and effectively work together, both for the long-term success of their marriage as well as the raising of their children.

Take life easy

Create time for relaxation and be intentional about it. Don't take life too seriously. Placing undue seriousness and pressure on yourself breeds stress that can negatively impact you and

AREAS OF MUTUAL RESPONSIBILITY

your family life, and your spouse and children will almost certainly be on the receiving end. As the years pass by, you'll notice interactions in your relationship becoming less physical. Therefore, you should rediscover the need for a love seat in the house and use it to stimulate interaction between each other. Form a habit of sitting close to each other as much as possible, sharing some jokes, and laughing hard as though no one is listening.

Being light-hearted is good for your marriage as well as your overall health. Such a relaxed atmosphere eliminates tension. Avoid anything that brings tension to your marriage. Always remember that a stressed person lacks the composure to respond or react well, even in the face of a slight provocation or upset.

Look after yourselves – physically, emotionally, and psychologically

Don't take your spouse or marriage for granted, as some couples tend to do with the passage of time. Make sure you remain as attractive as possible to your spouse and, even more importantly, to your self-confidence, happiness, and good mental well-being. Some Christians think that because their spouse is a Christian, they do not have any expectations regarding their spouse's looks. It seems as if some of the reasons are that, perhaps, "he is not going to divorce me anyway, so why should I make an effort to remain attractive to keep him?" I should lovingly let you know that you are dead wrong on that one!

> *Anything that takes your focus away from your marriage cannot be of God. God is not the author of confusion.*

AREAS OF MUTUAL RESPONSIBILITY

Set time aside for dates as regularly as possible

King Solomon wrote in the Song of Solomon: "I am my beloved's, and his desire is toward me. Come, my beloved, let us go forth to the field; let us lodge in the villages. Let us get up early to the vineyards; let us see if the vine has budded, whether the grape blossoms are open, and the pomegranates are in bloom. There I will give you my love. The mandrakes give off a fragrance, and at our gates are pleasant fruits, all manner, new and old, which I have laid up for you, my beloved." (Song of Solomon 7:10-13).

These romantic words read like something that was a vital and routine part of King Solomon and his wife's family life. King Solomon and his wife's mindset are excellent ideas that couples can emulate at any stage of their marriage—newly married or those who have been married for decades. These words highlight the need for couples to consciously look for opportunities that help them stick together ever so closely. It is necessary for any high-functioning marriage, especially in this day and age of fast-paced living.

This practice will help prevent you from drifting apart while, at the same time, affair-proofing your marriage. One way of achieving this exemplary level of intimacy may be for each of you to make a list of things you like to do or things you might want to try out together. It could be anything from antique hunting, garage sales, taking walks while holding hands, biking, fishing, visiting museums, watching sports either on TV or in an arena, shopping, gardening, reading, cooking, hiking, puzzles, and much more. There is so much that you can both do together as a couple.

AREAS OF MUTUAL RESPONSIBILITY

Once you have separately made your lists, compare them and see where there are overlaps. The overlaps indicate potential areas of common interest. Then find three to five things from your lists that you can regularly endeavor to do together. In fact, nothing should be off-limits. Go ahead, be adventurous, and try something that may not be familiar to both of you. Try something new and have a load of fun together. Having fun together as a couple makes it much harder for anyone or anything to come in between you.

> *The couple should make conscious efforts to date throughout the duration of their marriage, which is until death forces the couple to separate.*

Never forget at any time that your spouse remains your "date for life!" Therefore, going out regularly should not stop after a long courtship and a well-planned and successful wedding ceremony. You should make conscious efforts to date throughout the duration of your marriage—which is until death forces you to separate.

It seems to be common knowledge that women typically prefer to be responders when it comes to activities such as going out on dates. I know many of them who have confessed to being more comfortable with that role. Women (not all women, though) generally report that it feels awkward for them to initiate such events.

That leaves the responsibility to the husband, who must make sure that he gives his wife the opportunity to respond. Perhaps, as a couple, you can both schedule and put down some dates on your calendar well in advance, if necessary. That will ensure

AREAS OF MUTUAL RESPONSIBILITY

you are both committed to the dates. If you have young kids, get a babysitter, so it is just the two of you. It will be a great gift you can give your children. A cost-effective babysitting arrangement could be a friend with whom you can take turns babysitting each other's kids so that you can go out on dates with your spouse.

> *If you have kids, get a babysitter, so it is just the two of you. It will be the best gift you can give your children.*

Take your spouse's feedback seriously

If there is something you need to change, please do your best to change it. As we grow older and celebrate more wedding anniversaries, certain habits may creep into our lives without our knowledge. Some of such habits may be irritants to your spouse. If he or she points them out to you, you will do well to listen carefully without taking it personally. Working on such unwanted habits will ensure they are not coming between you and your spouse.

I think it is a sign of affection to point out a bad habit that you may spot in your spouse. That way, they can deal with it before it affects your relationship. Note that the habit may be trivial to you, but make no mistake; it may irritate your spouse. For example, I have heard some women complain about their husbands' habits of untidiness. They complained that their husbands were fond of leaving clothes on the floor or on the bed. That may not be a weighty issue for some people, but here I am, hearing about it from concerned wives.

AREAS OF MUTUAL RESPONSIBILITY

Communicate, communicate, and communicate

Personally, I firmly believe there can be no over-communication in a healthy marriage. If over-communication is possible, then I would recommend it in place of under-communication. When there is a communication break-down between a couple, a room may be created for assumptions, many of which are usually erroneous and unhealthy for the marriage.

Therefore, couples should communicate as much as possible because that will help to build trust in your marriage. As in all relationships, a couple with a history of good communication between them is most likely to know when a communication gap emerges between them. If it is, they will quickly nip it in the bud without allowing the gap to linger and even widen.

But effective communication means more than simply talking. Talking for the sake of it may well be regarded as noise-making. Therefore, couples should strive to communicate with the sole purpose of making a connection and staying connected. Connectedness is very important for any relationship that will last a long time. Connection takes people who are in a relationship to the soul of each other. It becomes easy to understand each other more intimately at that deep level.

Let me close this chapter by stressing that couples should carefully note that a *life of faith* or a *lifetime of marital bliss* doesn't mean the complete absence of challenges. Neither does it mean a life that is full of everything. There is probably no one whose life is entirely free of challenges or has everything that their heart has ever desired. Rather, it is the maintenance of faith and marital bliss amid needs or challenges that truly makes all the difference!

KEY TAKE AWAY

- At a minimum, parents must bequeath a *Life of Faith* and a *lifetime of marital bliss* to their children.

- It is a beautiful legacy for our children to grow up and say that their parents bequeathed a life of faith, so they are able to thrive despite the very challenging times.

- A couple that regularly prays with their children develops intimacy with God while exhibiting an attitude of dependence on God at the same time.

- It is important for children to learn early in their lives that prayer is the lifeline of a Christian. They should also understand prayer as a fundamental means of establishing intimacy with God.

- Learning how to fall in love with God's word happens simultaneously with falling in love with God himself.

- When a husband is loving his wife, he is automatically doing the best for his children at the same time.

- Some practical ways to achieve marital bliss:

    o Beware of the arrival of children.

    o Take life easy.

- Look after yourselves – physically, emotionally, and psychologically.

- Set time aside for dates as regularly as possible.

- Take your spouse's feedback seriously.

- Communicate, communicate, and communicate a bit more.

PART FIVE

The Anatomy of a Failed Marriage

- Chapter Eighteen: Biblical Position on Divorce
- Chapter Nineteen: Impact of Divorce on Society
- Chapter Twenty: Impact of Fatherlessness on Children
- Chapter Twenty-One: Emotional and Psychological Impact of Divorce
- Chapter Twenty-Two: When Divorce Becomes the only Option

"Divorce can save people from a bad marriage, but research has shown that it can also debilitate a society. Divorced adults are more likely to become impoverished while their children experience psychological and economic stress hindering their social development. According to the National Marriage Project, between 1960 and 2009, the divorce rate in the United States doubled; between 40 and 50 percent of newly married couples will either separate or divorce. With high divorce rates threatening social stability, the United Nations urges governments everywhere to adopt policies to reverse this trend."

- MICHELE VROUVAS

CHAPTER EIGHTEEN

BIBLICAL POSITION ON DIVORCE

"The Pharisees also came to Him, testing Him, and saying to Him, "Is it lawful for a man to divorce his wife for just reason?"

And He answered and said to them, "Have you not read that He who made them at the beginning made them male and female, and said, 'For this reason a man shall leave his father and mother and be joined to his wife, and the two shall become one flesh' So then, they are no longer two but one flesh. Therefore, what God has joined together, let not man separate. He said to them, "Moses, because of the hardness of your hearts, permitted you to divorce your wives, but from the beginning it was not so." (Matthew 19:3-6, 8).

This passage accounts for one of many encounters Jesus had with the Pharisees. We can see Jesus is very clear that divorce was not part of God's original plan when he was crafting the hallowed institution of marriage. There is no evidence anywhere in the Bible or elsewhere that God made a provision for divorce as part of marriage. In his response to a trap-setting question from the Pharisees, Jesus told them categorically that at the beginning, divorce was not on the cards. Jesus didn't mince words on the issue of divorce at all.

THE ANATOMY OF A FAILED MARRIAGE

Like all other depravities that we see in our world today, divorce came about because of the perversion of God's creation following the fall of man. As I alluded to in Chapter 9 of Volume 1, divorce is a creation of man, owing to his insistence on what he wants. That is, man insisting with no careful consideration of the consequences of what he thinks is good for him.

In this Part Five: The Anatomy of a Failed Marriage, we will take a closer look at the biblical perspective on divorce. We'll also examine the impact of fatherlessness on children. Furthermore, we'll also examine in detail the emotional and psychological impact of divorce on the couple involved and its impact on children. We'll also examine its impact on society as a whole. I have also included a few well-researched articles that have been written by people with demonstrated passion and expertise in this field.

> *Divorce is a creation of man owing to his insistence on what he wants.*

Malachi's account about divorce

> *"Yet you say, 'For what reason?' Because the Lord has been witness Between you and the wife of your youth, With whom you have dealt treacherously; Yet she is your companion And your wife by covenant. But did He not make them one, Having a remnant of the Spirit? And why one? He seeks godly offspring. Therefore, take heed to your spirit, And let none deal treacherously with the wife of his youth.*

THE ANATOMY OF A FAILED MARRIAGE

> *'For the Lord God of Israel says That He hates divorce, For it covers one's garment with violence,' Says the Lord of hosts. 'Therefore take heed to your spirit, That you do not deal treacherously.'"*
> (Malachi 2:14-16).

In his prophecy, Malachi, provides the above intriguing view of divorce. He is emphatic that God hates divorce. Hate, as we all know, is a very strong word. And it is probably because of its weight that the word "hate" is very sparingly used in the Bible to describe how God feels about something.

Let me briefly mention the view of a small percentage of Bible commentators regarding this passage. Those commentators have suggested that perhaps Prophet Malachi was talking about the children of Israel's lack of loyalty and commitment to their covenant relationship with God. That interpretation is probably not totally out of place. In fact, we can still use it to explain God's view on divorce.

Similarly, that scripture's most widely accepted interpretation is more fitting when applied to the human marriage institution. Both interpretations highlight the hurt that comes with any act of treachery and disloyalty. For instance, under the Old Covenant, the children of Israel suffered punitive consequences each time they separated themselves from the Lord God for other gods. It'll be right to describe their actions during such times as a divorce.

Divorce as an act of treachery

Malachi's prophecy describes divorce as an act of treachery, which has been used three times in these three short verses.

THE ANATOMY OF A FAILED MARRIAGE

According to the Merriam-Webster online dictionary, "treachery" means the violation of allegiance or of faith and confidence. We also see some emotional aspects of marriage when the Bible reminds husbands (and women too) that God is a witness between you and the wife of your youth, companion, and your wife by covenant. It also says that divorce covers one's garment with violence. Those are very strong words.

Prior to the past few decades, Malachi's prophecy seemed to suggest that husbands were primarily responsible for initiating divorce. But that is no longer the case in our world today, as we see a growing number of women initiating it too. Therefore, in biblical terms, whoever initiates divorce may be considered treacherous and violates the most fundamental human institution that God himself has created. It can be said that the inspiration Malachi received to write this lacked cognizance of some of the seemingly plausible reasons people opt for divorce today.

The phrase "violation of allegiance" is also noteworthy. The Bible rarely uses such strong language to drive home the meaning or significance of human acts or behaviors. That means we need to pay close attention when we come across a word or an expression that seeks to convey such a meaning in the Bible.

As humans, we know that trust or allegiance is absolutely necessary for building meaningful and enduring relationships. Trust is so important that I boldly invite you to show me any relationship in which there is no trust, and I will be happy to show you a relationship whose foundation is laid on pure sand, waiting for the slightest test for it to collapse.

THE ANATOMY OF A FAILED MARRIAGE

It goes without saying that for married couples, we all welcomed the opportunity to get married with great euphoria. You mustn't have forgotten the good feelings you had during courtship, the opportunities to meet the family of your to-be spouse for the first time, and the planning and the all activities leading to your wedding day. You proceeded to joyfully make the necessary sacrifices purely out of trust in the person you fell in love with.

Therefore, sadly, the implication of divorce is that all that sacrifice doesn't mean a thing anymore. This implication is true regardless of whether the man or woman is responsible for or has initiated the divorce. And as the Bible has said, it amounts to treachery.

> Trust is so important that I boldly invite you to show me any relationship in which there is no trust, and I'll be happy to show you a relationship whose foundation is laid on pure sand, waiting for the slightest test for it to collapse.

Divorce as a result of adultery

It's a well-known fact that adultery is among the top five causes of divorce. For that reason, I'm going to take a closer look at what the Bible says about it. I'll also delve deep into Jesus' teachings on forgiveness. In addition, I'll discuss Apostle Paul's teaching on grace and the issue of sin so that, hopefully, readers may find some help in developing a new perspective about adultery and divorce.

In one of his interactions with the Pharisees, Jesus said the following: "Furthermore, it has been said, whoever divorces his wife, let him give her a certificate of divorce. But I say to you that whoever divorce his wife for any reason except sexual immorality causes her to commit adultery; and whoever marries a woman who is divorced commits adultery" (Matthew 5:31-32).

It would seem here that Jesus was providing a condition when divorce might be allowed. That's when there is a proven case of sexual immorality against a married individual, whether a husband or a wife. Our Lord was clear on this point. However, I would humbly say that's true only when this passage is taken in isolation, without considering other momentous teachings of Jesus about forgiveness.

We know that for a well-rounded understanding and interpretation of scripture, it is always best to look at the whole Bible while carefully keeping in mind that no prophecy of scripture is of a standalone or private interpretation. This is according to 2 Peter 1:20.

Taking Peter's words into account, let's examine several other teachings of Jesus, starting with Matthew 18:21-35. In that passage, the Lord was answering Peter's question about forgiveness, which Peter had phrased this way, "Lord, how often shall my brother sin against me, and I forgive him? Up to seven times?" Jesus said to him, "I do not say to you, up to seven times, but up to seventy times seven..." In this passage, Jesus teaches two very powerful lessons about forgiveness. It's important to note that Jesus was teaching about offences and forgiveness in general. The offense may be as little as someone stealing one cent from your wallet or as grievous as a spouse cheating by committing adultery. In my view, the lesson Jesus teaches here

THE ANATOMY OF A FAILED MARRIAGE

is that, regardless of the gravity of the offense, the person who has offended you deserves your forgiveness.

The second lesson for us is what Jesus taught about the king who wanted to settle accounts with his servants in Matthew 18. During the process, the king discovered that one of the servants had mismanaged his 10,000 denarii (millions of dollars), which his master demanded that he should pay up. When the servant could not pay, his master commanded him to be sold, together with his entire household, as a price for what he owed.

The servant pleaded with his master, saying, "Please be patient with me, and I will do my best and pay all that I owe you." The master of the servant was moved with compassion and consequently released him and forgave him the whole debt.

That same servant went out to his own debtor, who only owed him 100 denarii (a few thousand dollars). Just like him, his debtor was unable to pay and started pleading with him to be patient with him and, in time, he would pay him. On the contrary, this servant refused to be compassionate towards his debtor. Rather, he insisted that his debtor must pay up everything that he owed and should pay up immediately.

Before long, word came to his master regarding the hardness of his wicked servant. And his master called him and addressed him quite directly, "You wicked servant! I forgave you all that debt because you begged me. Should you not also have had compassion on your fellow servant just as I had pity on you?"

Another important example is recorded in Luke 7, which contains the legendary account of that so-called "sinful" woman who came to meet Jesus where he was a guest in a Pharisee's home. Uninvited, the party crasher brought an alabaster flask of fragrant oil and stood at Jesus' feet behind him, weeping. She washed his feet with her tears and proceeded to wipe them with the hair of her head, and she also kissed his feet and anointed them with fragrant oil.

Now, when Jesus' host saw how this "sinful" woman was interacting with Jesus, he was very disappointed. Being a deeply religious man, he felt he was doing a nice thing by hosting Jesus in his home. Unfortunately, Jesus' interaction with the "sinful" woman led him to conclude that had Jesus been a prophet, he would have known what manner of woman she really was. Obviously, he expected Jesus to rebuke and even push her away from him.

Jesus immediately perceived Simon's thought process. Thus, he used the opportunity to teach one of his most profound lessons about forgiveness. In verse 41, he said, "There was a creditor who had two debtors. One owed him five hundred denarii, and the other fifty. And when they had nothing with which to repay, he freely forgave them both. Tell me, therefore, which of them will love him more?"

Simon answered and said, "I suppose the one whom he forgave more." And Jesus agreed with him that, indeed, he had answered correctly. Jesus implied that the greater the offense that is forgiven, the greater the appreciation from the offender. Therefore, when you are gracious enough to forgive your adulterous spouse, they will love and greatly appreciate you instead of taking you for granted and willfully continuing to do it.

THE ANATOMY OF A FAILED MARRIAGE

> *Jesus implied that the greater the offense that is forgiven, the greater the appreciation from the offender.*

Let me invite you to think about that for a moment. Cast your mind back to where you were before God sought, found, saved, and washed you clean from all your shortcomings. He went even further to give you his Spirit as a seal and now calls you his very own. Besides God's magnanimity that brought you into the saving knowledge of Jesus Christ, has it crossed your mind how often you have found yourself completely inadequate before him? Yet, God has consistently forgiven you. Make no mistake; like every other human being, you're inherently imperfect. That means that while you may not have committed adultery, you're most unlikely to have been altogether perfect.

> *Make no mistake; like every other human being, you are inherently imperfect. That means that while you may not have committed adultery, you are most unlikely to have been altogether perfect.*

But someone may ask, "Pastor Mannie, don't you think that in forgiving such an abominable offense which Jesus himself has given as a justification to divorce your spouse, won't it amount to condoning the atrocious act of adultery?" Others may ask, "Pastor Mannie, are you not advocating that a free license be given for married people to perpetuate adulterous behavior?" Not at all! In fact, far from it! I will be emphatic in saying that that is not how those who understand grace and the beauty of forgiveness behave.

Those who understand that they have committed a grave offense for which they have been forgiven appreciate it so much that such an unmerited favor made available to them effectively serves as a restrainer from making a practice of sin. In his epistle to the Romans, Paul penned these words, "Moreover the law entered that the offense might abound. *But where sin abounded, grace abounded much more*, so that as sin reigned in death, even so grace might reign through righteousness to eternal life through Jesus Christ our Lord." (Romans 5:20-21, emphasis added).

Paul further clarified to help those who may misconstrue his position by thinking that people were free to go ahead and sin as much as they wanted since unlimited grace was available to them. He clarified his position by posing this question in Romans 6:

> *"What shall we say then? Shall we continue in sin that grace may abound? Certainly not! How shall we who died to sin live any longer in it? Or do you not know that as many of us as were baptized into Christ Jesus were baptized into His death? Therefore we were buried with Him through baptism into death, that just as Christ was raised from the dead by the glory of the Father, even so we also should walk in newness of life"* (Romans 6:1-4).

Furthermore, John had this to say:

> *"Everyone who makes a practice of sinning also practices lawlessness; sin is lawlessness. You know that he appeared to take away sins, and in him*

> *there is no sin. <u>No one who abides in him keeps on sinning; no one who keeps on sinning has either seen him or known him.</u> Little children, let no one deceive you. Whoever practices righteousness is righteous, as he is righteous. <u>Whoever makes a practice of sinning is of the devil, for the devil has been sinning from the beginning</u>. The reason the Son of God appeared was to destroy the works of the devil. <u>No one born of God makes a practice of sinning</u>, for God's seed abides in him, and he cannot keep on sinning because he has been born of God"* (1 John 3:4-9, emphasis added).

Of course, I am not feigning any ignorance as to why only very few people are able to truly forgive and remain married to the same spouse following the act of adultery. Neither am I unable to imagine why most cases of adultery almost always irredeemably damage a marriage. I certainly do appreciate that the pain it causes can be very deep for those affected by it.

So, what is the conclusion regarding the issue of adultery and divorce? According to the scriptures we have discussed above, there should be no doubt in anyone's mind that a Christian with a good understanding of grace and the gift of forgiveness doesn't go on perpetuating himself or herself in sin. Rather, they are greatly humbled and overwhelmed with appreciation as they become more conscious of and are better positioned to flee every appearance of sin.

Finally, let me suggest that before anyone takes Matthew 5:31-32 and runs with it, they should take a deep breath, think hard, and ask themselves, "Will it be too expensive to forgive my spouse so that they can have another chance?" It is quite possible that many people who read or hear me share this perspective will consider it unprecedented and even revolutionary. And I agree, it probably is. But I strongly believe that doing so will surely go a long way in setting you apart as a magnanimous person.

Probably, there are still some who'll refer to this perspective as old school or not modern enough. For such people, I truly respect your views. However, I'll be happy to tell them that they're part of the primary audience for this book. The inspiration for this book is to help couples understand that though we're living in a fast-evolving twenty first world, taking a holistic look at the Word of God, I've concluded that marriage is one institution that shouldn't evolve. It's an area of human involvement that should be preserved and left as is. The fundamentals of marriage are supposed to remain the same as decades and centuries pass by.

There's no reason why the fundamentals of a properly constituted marriage today shouldn't be like those of a properly constituted marriage 1000 years ago. The two fundamentals that should define a properly constituted marriage are: first, a man leaves his father and mother and cleaves to his wife; the two should become one indivisible flesh; second, the two wholeheartedly build their lives together until death separates them.

However, let me emphatically state here that I'm not advocating that this should magically happen, nor am I suggesting that anyone should stay married at all costs, including at the expense of their lives. To that end, I've made my modest contribution to help couples achieve these two fundamentals by publishing volume 1 - Dating Etiquette for Singles, which aims to help singles become more intentional about dating; and, of course, this volume 2 that you are reading now. I'll also encourage couples to take full advantage of the wide array of tools and support systems that may be available to them. That support system and tools are what you'll need to help you manage your marital relationship from beginning to the end of it.

> *Finally, may I counsel that before anyone takes Matthew 5:31-32 and runs with it, they should take a deep breath, think hard, and ask themselves, "Will it be too expensive to forgive my spouse so that he can have another chance?"*

KEY TAKE-AWAYS

- God hates divorce.

- Divorce is man's creation. It was not part of God's original plan for marriage.

- There is a large amount of research showing that divorce negatively impacts societal cohesiveness.

- Stable, intact marriages are essential building blocks for a stable society.

- Jesus said that divorce may be permitted when a case of adultery is involved. However, with grace and magnanimity, adultery can be forgiven, and a marriage saved.

- The more grievous the offense, the greater the grace that's available to the offender.

- Forgiving an adulterous spouse means your heart is "large" enough to give an underserving offender a second chance.

CHAPTER NINETEEN

THE IMPACT OF DIVORCE ON THE SOCIETY

"American society may have erased the stigma that once accompanied divorce, but it can no longer ignore its massive effects. Mounting evidence in the annals of scientific journals details the plight of the children of divorce and clearly indicates not only that divorce has lasting effects, but that these effects spill over into every aspect of life."[15]

Did you know that the rate of divorce is trending towards an alarming rate to the extent that even the United Nations (UN), which is a completely secular organization, has decided to step in and is now urging governments everywhere to do whatever it takes to reverse the trend? See Michelle Vrouvas' quote at the beginning of Part Five above.

For instance, not too long ago, perhaps as recent as thirty years ago, a failed marriage was a shameful thing, especially among Christians. About thirty years ago, most Christian societies viewed divorce as something not so pleasant. It was considered a shameful situation, especially for the couple involved. But the feeling of shame was often extended to their immediate families as well. Obviously, such feelings were in keeping with what the Bible teaches, as shown in chapter eighteen above. As a result, in most cultures, some solid safeguards such as counseling, parents, and friends were available to support to ensure the marriage succeeded.

Some may have an argument similar to this one that I received from Salome as I shared this line of thought during a marriage retreat. She wrote me this note: "Back then, women didn't have any rights of their own. As a result, both physical and verbal abuse within a household were common. In the eyes of society, women were here to give birth, raise children, clean the house, and nothing more. They couldn't get an education or certain jobs. So, even if they did end their marriage, how would they survive and raise their kids without an income? And with the shame society placed on them, getting remarried would've been almost impossible, and their families would've abandoned them."

Salome's note contains some interesting perspectives. I responded to her viewpoints in two parts: The first is about the issue of rights. Clearly, society has evolved quite a bit, giving women many more rights these days. And men are also aware of these rights that women now have. So, to a large extent, wise men are careful in their dealings with their wives, knowing that it is illegal to trample on the rights of their wives. If he's ignorant or doesn't care, then the wife should remind him of those rights and advise him not to be seen to be taking laws into his own hands. Perhaps, everyone knows that there are consequences for anyone who takes laws into their own hands. If he still doesn't get it, then let the police know what's going on, and I am sure they will be happy to point you in the right direction.

The second part of my response is that education is almost an invaluable possession as it gives women the opportunity to aspire to their dream careers, which is a very good thing. However, as I've stated above, it's better to use one's rights, education, and great careers for the good of one's family life and not against it. I am essentially saying that a highly educated career woman should be in the best position to understand the value of an intact family and do all that is necessary to achieve it. To that end, I will suggest that it is not wise for one to arrogantly walk away from her marriage at the slightest irritation or conflict with the mindset that, after all, they are financially capable of providing for themselves.

Beyond the above two points, I'll add that no woman should be married primarily because she's illiterate, lacks employable skills, or doesn't have an income. Neither should any woman be in a marriage simply to try and protect her image or the image of her birth family. That'll be a miserable marriage. As I stated in *Dating Etiquette for Singles,* and with the additional content provided in this volume, you'd have enough tools to help you build a thriving and high-functioning marriage instead of staying in a marriage simply for the sake of it. A fun-filled marriage is very possible, but you must do what is necessary to achieve it. My recommended mindset for every couple to have is this: "I have thoughtfully decided to get married and stay married because I know that it's the right thing to do. And I know that there are going to be challenges, but I'll not allow such challenges to change my mindset."

> *My recommended mindset for every couple to have is this: "I've thoughtfully decided to get married and stay married because I know that it's the right thing to do. And I know that there are going to be challenges, but I'll not allow such challenges to change my mindset".*

THE ANATOMY OF A FAILED MARRIAGE

The longevity of subsequent marriages

I'm going to identify with the organizations and individuals who advocate that everyone's hands should be on deck to help our 21st-century world understand that divorce is hardly the best answer to marital challenges when all factors are carefully considered. According to the Divorce Strategies Group, emerging patterns, especially in North America, have shown that when the first marriage fails, subsequent marriages are more likely to fail, which is quite strange. *"Studies show the rate of divorce for first marriages has dropped to 40%. But the alarming statistic is the rate of failure for second marriages is 67% and for third marriages, it's a whopping 74%!"* [16]

The logical thought process is that people marrying after the failure of their first experience will have the "benefit" of knowing what kind of person to pick in their subsequent attempts. Unfortunately, reality has proven otherwise! Therefore, those who are hurriedly quitting their present marriages, hoping that a new marriage will make them happier and more fulfilled, should put on their thinking cap. They will likely end up with a rude shock and grave disappointment.

> *Therefore, those who are hurriedly quitting their first marriage, hoping that a second marriage will make them happier and more fulfilled, should put on their thinking caps.*

Let me also say that perhaps the time for sitting on the fence has elapsed. It's time for us all to step up and chip in our little contribution. I believe that, in the end, every action will count towards stemming the unfortunate tide of divorce.

THE ANATOMY OF A FAILED MARRIAGE

Patrick Fagan and Robert Rector, who have researched and written extensively for the Heritage Foundation, have this important summary recommendation about marriage.

"American society, through its institutions, must teach core principles: that marriage is the best environment in which to raise healthy, happy children who can achieve their potential and that the Family is the most important institution for social well-being. To set about the task of rebuilding a culture of Family based on marriage and providing it with all the protections and supports necessary to make intact marriages commonplace, federal, state, and local officials must have the will to act."[17]

Declan and Frances' story

A little over 15 years ago, Declan and Frances originally from one of the Caribbean Islands was having some challenges in their marriage. They were new immigrants to Canada, probably not up to a year. Declan had difficulty finding work in his field, but his wife was already gainfully employed. According to Frances, her husband was feeling very depressed and easily agitated. As a result, his state of mind was taking a toll on the whole family. In her desperate effort to save her marriage, she decided to seek counsel from their pastor.

After listening to Frances narrate her experience, her pastor asked her, "Are you not employed?" Frances answered in the affirmative. He then advised her to invite her husband to leave the house so she could take steps to file for divorce. "After all, you are employed and are capable of fending for yourself and your two-year-old son." Their pastor concluded. Frances was shocked to hear that from her pastor. According to her, she expected their pastor to bring them together to try and make peace.

THE ANATOMY OF A FAILED MARRIAGE

Meanwhile, Frances confided in my wife and me that it was not her husband's nature to be angry. She strongly felt that Declan was struggling with the issue of joblessness. She concluded that she was no longer comfortable attending that church. I was very pleased to hear that there are still many Christians out there who do not believe that divorce is the first and only solution when faced with marital challenges.

Once again, I think the church has an important responsibility to demonstrate exemplary leadership in an action-oriented manner in matters of marital stability. As the body of Christ, we need to help the world know that a high-functioning marriage is possible by how we lead our individual family lives. We also must prayerfully try to influence those who happen to come directly within our sphere of influence. This effort applies to every Christian, not just pastors only. If it must be in the mix, I believe divorce should always be seen as the last resort.

> I was very pleased to hear that there were still many Christians out there who do not believe that divorce is the first and only solution when faced with marital challenges.

It'll not be superfluous to say that a successful marriage is not something that just happens. It has to be crafted. It is the outcome of deliberate decisions coupled with actions to create a high-functioning marital relationship with your spouse. And that doesn't just happen. It comes through solid marriage education and an unwavering commitment.

We can also share our knowledge and experience with people around us. Requisite knowledge is very important if one is going to thrive in life. It's also evident that many of the marriage-destroying actions people take are because of their lack of essential knowledge about the marriage institution.

For example, after the crash in global oil prices in 2014, my wife and I ran into one of our attorney friends. As part of the usual small talk friends engage in when they see each other, we asked her how things were in her law practice.

"Things are okay, I will say." She responded.

I wasn't satisfied with her response because I like hearing that things are great, not just okay. So, I pressed a little further by asking her, "Is it just okay, not great?"

Then she added, "These days, lawyers who are having the best times are those doing Family Law."

I asked her why that was the case. She further told us that there was a huge rush for divorce services and that family lawyers could hardly keep up with the demand. That rush was partly due to the massive campaign by family lawyers for couples to come forward and file for divorce. Some of the lawn sign ads which had dotted Calgary's city streets during that time were very direct. One of such ads had words that read thus: "DIVORCE MADE EASY. CALL 403 XXX YYYY FOR HELP". Another read like this: "A-Z OF DIVORCE, HELP IS A PHONE CALL AWAY. CALL 403 XXX XXXX."

"What could have been the main motivating factor for all the rush to divorce?" That would be a good question to ask. The crash in oil prices saw tens of thousands of family men out of work. As I saw those lawn signs on many streets of the city of

THE ANATOMY OF A FAILED MARRIAGE

Calgary, I pondered the situation and couldn't help but ask, "Isn't it during such challenging times that couples are supposed to bond together ever so closely and hope for the best?" I guess, for many, that will be a naïve question to ask.

Certainly, I know that it is very easy to flow with the changing times, just as it is easy and safer to be quiet and avoid being identified with a particular position on important matters like marriage and divorce. As it is true with our prevailing politically correct culture, one may have a strong following, but I fear that it would be disingenuous and ultimately not good for the Christian faith that we profess and deeply cherish.

I will posit that if marriage is all about when money is flowing, life is good, and there is a great feeling of security, then what is the meaning of "for better, for worse" marriage vows that couples probably recited during their wedding? Unless the vows were recited only for formality with no intention of living them out.

> Besides, I feel marriage is too important to be lamely dragged into the politically-correct culture of our time.

Let me appeal that no one should get me wrong on this one. I am not in any way minimizing the importance or even the necessity of financial security for a married couple. Without any doubt, we all need security. Certainly, life is merrier when we have the good things that make us feel safe and secure. I am simply suggesting that couples should not abandon their marriage only for the simple fact that those good material things are missing or in short supply.

THE ANATOMY OF A FAILED MARRIAGE

> *I am not in any way minimizing the importance or even the necessity of financial security for a married couple.*

In fact, it is unwise for anyone to aspire to build his or her marriage on an abundance of financial or material things. Experience has shown that marital relationships founded purely on material things will almost always collapse if, for any reason, those things are no longer present. Material things should be seen as mere icing on the cake, not the cake itself. As it's commonsense, no one leaves the cake and goes after the icing!

This is consistent with what our Lord Jesus said, in Luke 12:15, he stated that a man's life does not consist in the abundance of things he possesses. Jesus was basically saying that who you are and what motivates you should not be centered on the abundance of things you possess. This is true because those whose life is centered on the abundance of things they possess can be likened to those who are building their treasures here on earth with no serious thought about eternity.

> *As important and necessary as material things are for comfort and security, a marital relationship founded on the presence of those things will almost always collapse if, for any reason, those things are no longer present.*

KEY TAKE AWAY

- Everyone (singles, married, churches, corporate organizations, etc.) has a part to play in ensuring that intact families remain the norm in our world today.

- Experience clearly shows that:
    - marriage is the best environment in which to raise healthy, happy children who can achieve their potential.
    - family is the most important institution for social well-being.

- Those looking forward to their next marriage as they consider divorce should think hard and long because, after the first marriage, subsequent ones are known to be even less likely to succeed. Therefore, you may be better off putting your best effort into your first marriage to make it thrive.

- Married couples should make every effort to keep their marriage vows in view as they grow and mature into their marathon married life.

- An abundance of material substances is like icing on the cake. While your marriage, on the other hand, is like the real cake. Don't let the quest for material substances decide if you'll divorce or remain married.

- Use every intervention at your disposal to avoid the failure of your marriage.

CHAPTER TWENTY

THE IMPACT OF FATHERLESSNESS ON CHILDREN

"A boy needs a father to show him how to be in the world. He needs to be given swagger, taught how to read a map so that he can recognize the roads that lead to life and the paths that lead to death, how to know what love requires, and where to find steel in the heart when life makes demands on us that are greater than we think we can endure." – Ian Morgan Cron

In general, both father and mother make significant and unique contributions to their children's upbringing. However, the unwritten role of fathers in a child's upbringing is indisputably unique and amazing. From my experience, I would say that the role starts right from the pregnancy stage.

One may ask, "What parental responsibility can a father discharge to an unborn child?" A lot! I'll say. At a minimum, while the mother is still carrying the pregnancy, the father can take steps to faithfully pray for the unborn child by laying hands on his wife's stomach.

This is a critical time to pronounce the appropriate Word of God upon the yet-to-be-born child. Constantly praying for a well-rounded fetus' development throughout the duration of the pregnancy is important. This practice has its basis in the Bible. God told prophet Jeremiah, "Before I formed you in the womb I knew you; Before you were born I sanctified you; I ordained you a prophet to the nations" (Jeremiah 1:15). With the understanding of this scripture in mind, fathers should be spiritually sensitive enough to get involved in their children's lives even before they are born. That's being spiritually strategic in the discharge of your parental responsibility.

Parental role of fathers and mothers

Recently, I came across the table below which I find interesting. The table gives some important clues why both parents are important in the heathy and balanced upbringing of a child.

Mother	Father
Loves till you close your eyes	Loves without an expression in his eyes
Introduces you to the world	Introduces the world to you
Gives you life	Gives you a living
Makes sure you are not starving	Makes sure you understand the value of starving
Personifies care	Personifies responsibility
Protects you from a fall	Teaches you to get up from a fall
Teaches you from her own experience	Teaches you to learn from your own experience

Table I – Mother and Father's Parental Roles

THE ANATOMY OF A FAILED MARRIAGE

Looking at the father's column from this table, it becomes easy to see why a child who grows up without a father or father's active involvement may negatively impact their ability to grow up into well-rounded adults. And this will be a result of a lack of the critical life skills that a father typically impacts.

As the child is born and growth and development start, fathers are responsible for instilling discipline and moral uprightness in their children. I am not sure why, but I know that when it comes to discipline, no one will dispute the fact that children tend to take their fathers more seriously than their mothers. It is interesting how the father's presence alone greatly influences a child's behavior and general demeanor.

Mothers, on the other hand, impact emotional, loving, and caring traits into their children. That's where the balance comes from – both parents giving to their children based on the natural abilities that God has endowed them with. Only a very few parents, if any, can effectively play these dual roles in the upbringing of their children. In other words, no mother can be a great mom and a great dad. Neither is there a super dad out there who can be a great father and a great mother simultaneously.

I congratulate both fathers and mothers for bringing those beautiful children into the world. You have done well by electing to be parents. But I will quickly add that working selflessly together as a team to raise them is certainly the most important responsibility of your life. In recognition of that fact, I will hasten to single out fathers to never consider fleeing and abandoning those beautiful children for any reason.

THE ANATOMY OF A FAILED MARRIAGE

Fathers must never forget that those children did not choose to come into this world. They are your seeds. You introduced the world to them, and you must stay and be a father to them. When you abandon them, you create a gaping hole in their lives that no one else will be good enough to adequately fill. Mothers also shouldn't chase their husbands away from the family home for any reason. This can happen through nagging, demeaning, verbal and psychological harassment, and so on.

In any case, even if there is a great man out there who is willing to step in and be a father to your children, why would you want to abdicate such a privileged and very rewarding responsibility to another person? Don't do it! In case you are unaware, the world cannot afford one more child growing up without a father! And if you are reading this book as a runaway father, let me appeal to you to go back home and be truly present in the lives of your children.

> In any case, even if there is a great man out there who is willing to step in and be a father to your children, why would you want to abdicate such a privileged and very rewarding responsibility to another person?

Several years ago, Patrick Fagan undertook a study about the impact of the father's absence in the life of a growing child. In his study titled *"The Real Root Causes of Violent Crime: The Breakdown of Marriage, Family and Community*[19]*"*, he documented these findings:

- Over the past thirty years, the rise in violent crimes parallels the rise in families abandoned by fathers.
- High-crime neighborhoods are characterized by high concentrations of families abandoned by fathers.

THE ANATOMY OF A FAILED MARRIAGE

- State-by-state analysis by Heritage scholars indicates that a 10 percent increase in the percentage of children living in single-parent homes leads typically to as much as seventeen percent increase in juvenile crimes.
- The rate of violent teenage crimes corresponds with the number of families abandoned by fathers.

It will be a rare occurrence for anyone to be a good parent but lead an unstable marriage. Good parenting and a good marriage are often found together.

Key reasons for the devastating impact of fatherlessness on children

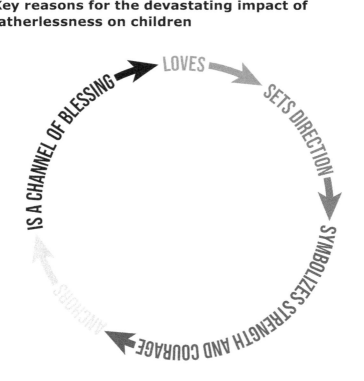

Figure II: Father's Responsibility Cycle

THE ANATOMY OF A FAILED MARRIAGE

The picture above shows what I refer to as the "Father's Responsibility Cycle." It represents some of the key roles a father performs to ensure his children's healthy and balanced upbringing. This cycle shows the gap that will result in a child's lopsided development without his father. Therefore, it should not come as a surprise why, quite often, the lives of children who are raised largely in the absence of their father tend to lack some important life skills. Each of these responsibilities has been discussed below.

A father loves.

As shown in Table I above, the love of a father, though deep, is usually expressionless. For that reason, a father's love is not always obvious to an undiscerning young child. Some children often misunderstand their father's love as devoid of emotions, which is not true. How the father displays emotions just differs from how the mother shows hers. Nonetheless, as God has designed it, when that so-called "father's emotionless" love is lacking in a child's life, it leaves an indelible scar on their overall development.

Here are a few ways that a father shows his love to his children:

Discipline: "We do not enjoy being disciplined. It is painful at the time, but later, after we have learned from it, we have peace, because we start living in the right way" (Hebrews 12:11).

A child who grows up with a loving and competent father will likely understand the meaning and importance of discipline. When a father disciplines his son or daughter, he does so out of love, not a lack of it. That is precisely what we learn from our heavenly Father. He disciplines those whom he loves. We learn this from the book of Proverbs: "My son, do not despise the chastening of the Lord, Nor detest His correction; For whom the Lord loves He corrects, Just as a father the son in whom he delights" (Proverbs 3:11-12).

And in Hebrews, the Bible admonishes us to "Endure hardship as discipline; God is treating you as his children. For what children are not disciplined by their father?" (Hebrews 12:7).

These passages essentially tell us that if a child is not receiving discipline from his or her father, such a child should not be happy because it means he is illegitimate or his father does not love him. That means children who have fathers who care enough to discipline them should count themselves truly blessed.

One more reason a father should be present for his children is to lovingly correct their undesirable behavior. And when the child learns from the correction, he truly enjoys peace. This means that he applies the lessons learned from the correction and as a result avoids the same mistake which then leads to a good and a peaceful life.

Strictness – A loving father will not allow his children to always have their way because doing so sets them up for failure later in life. A simple but fitting example is when some fathers will hardly allow their children to go for a sleepover, no matter how upset they might feel about it. Some who allow sleepovers do so by carefully picking and choosing where and when their children can go for a sleepover. A loving father will firmly say no when he is not sure of the family that his children want to go to for a sleepover. Fathers know all too well that sometimes children may be exposed to some experience, such as molestation, that will have a negative impact on them for the rest of their lives.

Sacrifice – Out of love, the father does everything he can to ensure his family has what it needs. That's the example God has shown us as our heavenly Father. He sacrificially sent his Son, to die in our place, to take away our sins. At some point in the life of a father, all that matters is his children; nothing else does. Such a sacrifice is usually made in the spirit of love for his children.

Age-appropriate giving - Usually, children will not understand why their father will not allow them to have certain things at a certain age. This is because a loving father knows when the time is right for his children to have certain things. These can be as simple as toys or as significant as weekly monetary allowances. For example, for obvious reasons, no matter how wealthy a father may be, it will probably be ill-advised to place his twelve-year-old child on a $1,000 weekly allowance. Jesus said, "If you then, being evil, know how to give good gifts to your children, how much more will your Father who is in heaven give good things to those who ask Him!" (Matthew 7:11). Certainly, there are "bad" gifts that would turn out to be a curse if given to children before they are mature enough to use such gifts wisely to their benefit.

A father sets direction for his family

"Life doesn't come with an instruction book — that's why we have fathers." - H. Jackson Browne

THE ANATOMY OF A FAILED MARRIAGE

The meaning of Browne's statement is obvious. Life doesn't have an instruction or reference manual. Although we have the Bible, more often than not, children find it a lot easier to look up to their fathers for direction and guidance. That is why somebody anonymously defined a father as someone children look up to no matter how tall they grow. At the family level, the father is responsible for setting directions for how things should be done. This includes setting the direction for spiritual and financial matters as well.

Hear what God said of Abraham: "Shall I hide from Abraham what I am doing, since Abraham shall surely become a great and mighty nation, and all the nations of the earth shall be blessed in him? For I have known him, in order that he may command his children and his household after him, that they keep the way of the Lord, to do righteousness and justice, that the Lord may bring to Abraham what He has spoken to him" (Genesis 18:17-19).

It's important to note the certainty with which God said, "for I know him, ... he will command his children and his household after him." God is still looking for fathers that he can say, "I know him. He is capable of raising godly children who will keep the way of the Lord." I believe that's a good challenge for fathers to welcome wholeheartedly.

In Paul's first letter to the Thessalonians, he said, "As you know how we exhorted, and comforted, and charged every one of you, *as a father does his own children*, that you would walk worthy of God who calls you into His own kingdom and glory" (1 Thessalonians 2:11-12). Italics are mine for emphasis. That is the direction-setting responsibility of a father for his family.

THE ANATOMY OF A FAILED MARRIAGE

"Being a great father is like shaving. No matter how good you shaved today, you have to do it again tomorrow." Reed Markham

Reed was simply implying that you don't retire from being a father. What changes is how you go about performing that role. When your children are toddlers, you parent them appropriately for their age. When they become teenagers, you parent them as teenagers. You are still their father when they are young adults or undergraduates. And as they mature and get married, your role as a father takes a different shape. Then you grow to become a grandpa, and the various stages evolve and go on and on until you pass away.

A father symbolizes strength and courage

"I cannot think of any need in childhood as strong as the need for a father's protection." – Sigmund Freud

Every child needs to feel safe and well-protected, in the home and, indeed, elsewhere. And naturally, children look up to their fathers for this much-needed protection. As a result of this expectation, the father must demonstrate the capacity and courage to meet his children's need for protection. In human terms, he is like a defense shield for his children. Deuteronomy says, "Then I said to you, 'Do not be terrified, or afraid of them. The Lord your God, who goes before you, He will fight for you, according to all He did for you in Egypt before your eyes, and in the wilderness where you saw how the Lord your God carried you, *as a man carries his son*, in all the way that you went until you came to this place'" (Deuteronomy 1:29-31).

THE ANATOMY OF A FAILED MARRIAGE

A father is his family's anchor

"A family needs a father to anchor it." – L. Tom Perry

To anchor something is to secure it firmly in position or to provide it with a firm basis or foundation. Other words that are often used when describing 'anchor' are *security, stability, calmness*, or being *grounded*. Putting these words together, we get a sense of the father's indomitable role in his family. He ensures that his family is secure, stable, and firmly grounded. We know that in life, circumstances are bound to come that will likely be unsettling for some people. In such situations, the father steps in and declares, "Calm down, everybody; it's going to be okay." Sometimes, he won't even bother to say a word, but his calm and stable demeanor alone conveys the reassuring message that there is absolutely no cause for alarm.

To provide security, the father first needs to be secure; to provide stability, he needs to be stable himself. He needs to be stable spiritually, physically, emotionally, psychologically, and morally. Similarly, to be calm and grounded, he must exude those qualities.

A father is a channel of blessing for his children

"Children, obey your parents in the Lord, for this is right. "Honor your father and mother," which is the first commandment with promise: "that it may be well with you and you may live long on the earth" (Ephesians 6:1-3).

In this passage, Paul echoes Exodus 20:12. When a child honors his father, God releases a special blessing as a result. That means that when a father is not available in the lives of his children,

THE ANATOMY OF A FAILED MARRIAGE

they will not be able to leverage that special avenue to get the blessing that should be theirs. Stated differently, the father's absence deprives his children of the opportunity to honor him and be blessed in return.

From the foregoing, it is therefore, no surprise that when a father abandons his family, the impact on the children is usually very great. Evidently, such people struggle through life from one level of dysfunction to another. For these reasons and more, no matter how difficult things might be, fathers should do whatever they can to ensure they lead intact family lives. It is the right thing to do. In the end, it will be fulfilling for them, just as it is good for their children, who will go on and thrive in life.

A Hallmark's story

A good friend of mine told me the following story, which further explains the anger in people who grew up without their fathers. The story goes like this:

> *"In a certain American prison, Hallmark offered free cards to inmates that wanted to send cards to their mothers on Mother's Day. Hallmark had to go back and get more cards because the demand was so high. The card maker decided it was such a success they would do the same for Father's Day. Unfortunately, not one card was used."*

From the father's roles described above, it is not hard to understand why people whose lifestyle has taken them to prison will not bother to send a card to their father on Father's Day. Most probably, they were angry because they all traced their problems to the absence of their fathers. This Hallmark experience with inmates can be interpreted this way: "Thank you, mom, for being there for us. You did your best. If only our dads were around to play their fatherly role in raising us up, we wouldn't be in jail."

Besides, it might be possible that most of the inmates did not even know who their father was. Some of them may not have even seen their fathers since their birth. And those who did obviously could not justify why their father deserved a card from them on Father's Day.

KEY TAKE AWAY

- Fathers and mothers are both critical in ensuring their children's healthy and balanced upbringing.

- No super mother is capable of effectively playing the role of a father.

- Children who grow up without a father are more likely to commit crimes.

- Crime-infested neighborhoods in many North American cities are typically dominated by households that have been abandoned by their fathers.

- The reward of fatherhood is too attractive to be abandoned by any sensible father.

- A household without a father is like a ship without an anchor – it is likely to be insecure, unstable, and unhinged.

- Boys who grow up without a father stand the risk of also abandoning their family when they grow up.

CHAPTER TWENTY-ONE

EMOTIONAL AND PSYCHOLOGICAL IMPACT OF DIVORCE

Without fear of contradiction, I will suggest that the level of trust that marriage demands is unparalleled by any other type of human relationship. I believe it is for this reason that victims of divorce often suffer such an unfathomable weight of emotional and psychological damage. Unfortunately, human emotions or psychological experiences are hardly visible. One only needs to listen to the heart of a victim of divorce to appreciate the gravity of the pain that comes with it.

A woman who went through a divorce once described it as the gravest of all rejections. That's right! Many who have experienced divorce have confessed that it is a very terrible form of rejection. She went further to emphasize that, "although there are all kinds of rejections, the pain that comes with divorce is in its own class. Ask anybody who has gone through divorce, and they will tell you that it is difficult to describe accurately." She concluded.

Another touching confession came from a neighborhood acquaintance. One day, we were chatting about current affairs, and unexpectedly, we veered into talking about family.

THE ANATOMY OF A FAILED MARRIAGE

And I asked him if he had children, to which he answered, "I am not even married, let alone have children." He noticed that I was a bit surprised.

"How come?" I asked him. He went further to say, "Having survived a heart-wrenching divorce experience, I will never ever get married again. Never!" He said very emphatically.

More often than not, people think of divorce simply as a couple who have irreconcilable differences and somewhat or mutually agree that the best way forward is to go their separate ways. Such thinking sounds simplistic and benign. The proven impact of divorce on its victims and the general society is neither simple nor benign. I have to stress here that making divorce appear simple and harmless does not minimize its far-reaching impact on its direct victims and the general society.

> I have to stress here that, making divorce appear simple and harmless does not minimize its far-reaching impact on its direct victims and the general society.

The following is a beautiful and well-researched article, which was written by Amy Desai for "Focus on the Family".

Understanding the impact divorce

"Psychologist Judith Wallerstein followed a group of children of divorce parents from the 1970s into the 1990s. She expected to find that kids bounce back from divorce, interviewing them 18 months, 5, 10, 15 and 25 years after the divorce. What she found was amazing: twenty-five years after the divorce, these children continued to experience substantial expectations of failure, fear of loss, fear of change and fear of conflict.[1] Twenty-five years!

Forming romantic relationships

The children in Wallerstein's study were especially challenged when they began to form their own romantic relationships. As Wallerstein explains, "Contrary to what we have long thought, the major impact of divorce does not occur during childhood or adolescence. Rather, it rises in adulthood as serious romantic relationships move center stage.... Anxiety leads many [adult children of divorce] into making bad choices in relationships, giving up hastily when problems arise, or avoiding relationships altogether."[2]

Other researchers confirm Wallerstein's findings.[3] Specifically, compared to kids from intact homes, children who experienced their parents' divorce view premarital sex and cohabitation more favourably.[4] (This is disturbing news given that cohabiting couples have more breakups, greater risk of domestic violence[5] and are more likely to experience divorce.[6]) Behind each of these statistics is a life – a child, now an adult, still coping with the emotions brought on by the divorce.

Lingering effects

Lilly is not a high school dropout, or drug user. She is, in fact, a college graduate who is quite successful in her career. But her parents' divorce haunts her to this day: "My parents divorced almost 30 years ago when I was 12 years old.

THE ANATOMY OF A FAILED MARRIAGE

Today, I am married with my own family but still feel the effects of my parents' decision to divorce. As with most divorce situations, my father left the home. I've never gotten over the feeling that he abandoned me in my most urgent hour of need. Even though my father continued to see me on weekends and during 'visitation' periods, occasional interactions could not heal this deep sense of abandonment.

As an adult, whenever I sense that someone I trust is not present for me, it rekindles this abandonment issue with my father. Still to this day, I think of the divorce and cannot understand how a man could pack his bags and walk away from his children. He would say he walked out of the home, not our lives, but that's not how I saw it."

Children will never fully understand

Parents considering divorce need to know that no matter how much they "explain the divorce" to their children, the children will never understand, even 30 years later.

Lilly's story could have been written by almost any child of divorce. As Wallerstein put it, "The kids [in my study] had a hard time remembering the pre-divorce family... but what they remembered about the post-divorce years was their sense that they had indeed been abandoned by both parents, that their nightmare [of abandonment] had come true."[7]

Parents tend to want to have their own needs met after a divorce – to find happiness again with someone new. But not only do the old problems often resurface for the adults, new problems are added for the children. As Wallerstein observed, "It's not that parents love their children less or worry less about them, it's that they are fully engaged in rebuilding their own lives – economically, socially and sexually. Parents and children's needs are often out of sync for many years after the breakup."[8] Children again feel abandoned as parents pursue better relationships and a new life.

Effects of remarriage

Feelings of abandonment and confusion are only compounded when one or both parents find a new spouse. A second marriage brings complications and new emotions for children – not to mention new step-siblings, step-parents and step-grandparents, who are often in competition for the parent's attention. (And the adjustment can be even more difficult because it is the adults who choose new families, not the children.) Lilly expressed it this way:

"My loss was magnified as my father remarried and adopted a new 'family.' Despite attempts on my part to keep in touch, we live in different cities, and his life now revolves around his new family with infrequent contact with me. This has only increased the feelings of abandonment and alienation from the divorce. And the high rate of second-marriage divorces can leave children reeling from yet another loss."

Full "recovery" is nearly impossible for children because of the dynamic nature of family life. While you and your ex-spouse's lives may go on separately with relatively little thought, your children will think about their loss almost every day. And 25 years after the fact, they will certainly be influenced by it. Life itself will remind them of the loss at even the happiest moments.

THE ANATOMY OF A FAILED MARRIAGE

As Earll explains: "Children never get over divorce. It is a great loss that is in their lives forever. It is like a grief that is never over. All special events, such as holidays, plays, sports, graduations, marriages, births of children, etc., bring up the loss created by divorce as well as the family relationship conflicts that result from the "extended family" celebrating any event."[9]

What parents see as a quick way out often results in emotional damage that the children will carry for 30 years, or more. Divorce is no small thing to children. It is the violent ripping apart of their parents, a loss of stability, and often a complete shock. While we often think of children as resilient, going through such trauma is a lot to ask of our kids.

It is our hope that reading this section has helped you better understand your children's perspective. In light of the fact that most marriages heading for divorce can be salvaged and turned into great marriages, parents should take a long pause before choosing divorce. While it may seem like a solution to you, it's not an easy way out for you or your kids."

"© 2001 by Focus on the Family. All rights reserved. Reprinted with *permission.*"

Here is what Sally Greene, who experienced the effect of divorce on adult children firsthand, had to say. Sally's parents divorced when she was eighteen years old. "When my parents divorced, it hurt me deeply. That pain was compounded when they were dishonest with me, talked negatively about the other, or expected me to take the place of a counsellor…"

Wallerstein's findings and the scenario Sally has described above play out all the time. Parents whose marriages have gone sour

THE ANATOMY OF A FAILED MARRIAGE

always paint each other so negatively just to try and make themselves look right and their spouses wrong. And very often, their negative talk has very little truth in it.

Unfortunately, such couples seem to hardly realize that children care less about who is right and who is wrong. The disputing parents need to be aware that all their children care about is that their parents are adults who should grow up and be able to work through their differences instead of relentlessly bad-mouthing each other in front of their innocent children. It is so unfortunate how leaving a marriage is fraught with guilt, and people will abandon truth and reality to try to clear their conscience and justify an exit.

In fact, colloquially, the children are screaming at the top of their voices and saying: "Stop all this nonsense talk about divorce and bad-mouthing each other. The resulting psychological and emotional trauma is taking a toll on me, and I can't bear it for one moment longer." Parents need to take a step back and listen to hear them.

KEY TAKE AWAY

- Many victims of divorce have agreed that it is the worst form of rejection.

- Studies show that children who experienced divorce continue to experience substantial expectations of failure, fear of change, and fear of conflict well into adulthood.

- Divorce leaves indelible emotional and psychological scars on its victims for decades. That includes moms, dads, and children.

- Often, couples heading towards divorce tell lies against each other to justify their exit, which is unfortunate from a child's perspective.

- Studies have shown that children will never understand their parents' reasons for opting to divorce.

- As a parent, when opting for a divorce, kindly take the impact of your decision on your children into account.

CHAPTER TWENTY TWO

WHEN DIVORCE BECOMES THE ONLY OPTION

If you have carefully read this book up to this point, you would have realized that divorce is not a particularly great option for marital relationships. As I have shown in the preceding pages, this fact has been echoed by many organizations, including the United Nations, American Family Heritage, and Focus on the Family, and individuals who have taken it upon themselves to help couples sustain their intact marriages. And above all else, the Bible, which is our highest authority, also says so.

I hope that the embellished flamboyance with which some have sought to associate divorce has been exposed for what it really is. As previously mentioned, the statistics show that your greatest chance of having a successful marriage is with your first marriage. After the first marriage, subsequent marriages are less likely to be successful. Hopefully, that will be good food for thought, and will make every couple invest everything they've got into their first marriage instead of giving it up so hastily.

THE ANATOMY OF A FAILED MARRIAGE

> *If you have carefully read this book up to this point, you would have realized that divorce is not particularly a great option for marital relationships.*

That said, the choice is still yours to make if, after doing everything within your power to make your marriage work, you are still unsuccessful. That is, you have come to a point where you have decided that divorce is the only choice left for you. Deciding to end a marriage is fairly easy for some people. However, some are often confused about when it's the right time for them to actually take that final critical step. If you have come to that point, I'll recommend that in cases where you still have the choice to give yourself a little more time, you seriously consider doing so. Give yourself some extra time to ensure you've exhausted all options to make things work.

Given the far-reaching negative impact divorce can have on all those involved, at least six months will not be too much to give yourself and your marriage. As you wait during this extra time, continue to leverage all the available support systems at your disposal, while keeping an open mind to the possibility that a turnaround may just happen in the process. And when it does happen, your marriage will receive a fresh impetus similar to or even greater than the one you started your marriage with.

Time has been proven to be a good healer, especially at the emotional level. That's why I'll strongly suggest that no one should rush into taking that final step. If you give yourself some time, you would likely heal from whatever may be leading you to walk out of your marriage. That's what that period of at least six months will help you achieve. Think very carefully

THE ANATOMY OF A FAILED MARRIAGE

and hard before you call a divorce lawyer to start the paperwork for a divorce!

Ahemen and Angelica's story

This young Southern Ontario couple got married after dating for about six months. About one year into their marriage, nothing seemed to work. Ahemen and Angelica where always arguing over everything. By the time their marriage was fifteen months old, they mutually agreed they needed a break from each other. About a year after they separated, they decided that divorce was the best option for them. But while they were in the process of deciding who their lawyer will be, Ahemen called Angelica and told her what he had been thinking over the three previous weeks. He asked Angelica if she would mind a weekend get-away. Angelica was a bit hesitant what the suggestion meant.

After thinking about it for a couple of days, she accepted the offer. Then Ahemen called and booked a cottage on the Muskoka Lake. On their second night together, Ahemen told Angelica how he had unsuccessfully tried to articulate the real reasons why they were separated and now planning to permanently end their marriage altogether. He then asked Angelica if she was exactly sure what were her real reasons for their plan to divorce. Funny enough, she too was unable to come up with a single cogent reason why their first year was turbulent and now in the process of divorcing.

The couple then decided that they still loved each other and it was immature and unwise to divorce if they couldn't even convince themselves exactly why. They agreed to give their marriage another chance. That was fifteen years ago and this couple is still married.

THE ANATOMY OF A FAILED MARRIAGE

Many couples in struggling marriages can have a story similar to this one. It is fairly common to see warring couples unable to articulate the significance of the issues that're making them to contemplate divorce. Often, the key turnaround occurs when they're willing to talk and allow reason to prevail so they can give their marriage a chance.

KEY TAKE AWAY

- If you have to divorce, be completely satisfied that you have done everything humanly possible to save your marriage.

- Once you have determined that divorce is the only option available to you, please give yourself some extra time to brood over the critical decision you're about to make. This extra time is to give your marriage one last chance.

- Sometimes, miracles do happen when you least expect them. Such could happen to your marriage during that extra time.

- When the miracle of restoration eventually happens, you'll truly be starting afresh with enthusiasm and energy similar to the one you had as a newlywed. And what a joy that will be!

PART SIX

There is Hope and a Future

- Chapter Twenty-Three: Hope for the Divorced
- Chapter Twenty-Four: Hope for the Fatherless Child

"And hope does not put us to shame, because God's love has been poured out into our hearts through the Holy Spirit …"

(Romans 5:5 NIV).

CHAPTER TWENTY-THREE

HOPE FOR THE DIVORCED

For various reasons, many beautiful couples have found themselves out of their marriages. According to Goldhart & Associates law firm in Toronto, Canada, these reasons range from money, infidelity, lack of compatibility, and going into marriage without a proper understanding of what marriage entails. Often, this includes a lack of understanding of marital responsibilities, a spouse's personality, value system, and sociocultural background.

Some have been divorced because shortly after getting married, they discovered that they knew very little about the person they married. And the new discovery of their spouse's real personality presents such a rude shock that they cannot handle it. Also, not many women are tolerant of abusive relationships. So, when they discover that their spouse is abusing them, they prefer to leave the marriage rather than stay. Some people have divorced their spouses because they could not have children together for certain biological reasons.

Yet, few have said they were simply tired of their partner, and they confessed feeling like someone who was bound with fetters in their marriage. As a result, they decide to divorce to gain independence. I am also aware of some cases where women have been deemed misfits in their new families, so much so that the relationship simply did not work out, and unfortunately, they had to leave. The reasons why people divorce are truly many!

As much as divorce has become common today, most Christian couples I know who have divorced report a deep sense of regret that their marriage failed. I have heard some divorced individuals say, "It never crossed my mind that I would experience divorce in my marriage." Some say this with tears in their eyes.

> *As much as divorce is becoming increasingly common in our day, the majority of Christian couples that I know who have divorced report a deep sense of regret that their marriage failed.*

Clearly, **Part Five – The Anatomy of a Failed Marriage** above has highlighted the physical and socio-economic cost of divorce as a reality that affects victims of divorce. We've also seen that divorce is known to be an important cause of societal instability. Therefore, if perhaps you are in your n^{th} (that is, second, third, fourth, fifth, etc.) marriage, I would like to assure you that there is still hope for you. You can recover from the damaging impact of divorce. You are of great value and are highly appreciated.

I have to write this chapter to address the concern of many couples who have divorced and are wondering if they are still Christians and whether they will ever be in right standing with God or not. Some divorced people have also wondered where they fit into God's plan for their lives as individuals. While divorce is arguably a very unsettling life event with far reaching ramifications, I believe with all of my heart that you are still a Christian, and you haven't lost your salvation by virtue of your status as a divorced person. In fact, I am happy to remind you that God's love for you has not diminished by any stretch of the imagination.

Some may ask, "If a divorced person is still a Christian, why then is the Bible discouraging it?" Somebody once asked, "If a divorced person is still a Christian and can go to heaven, isn't that viewpoint encouraging divorce?" The answer is "No." That viewpoint is not meant to encourage divorce in any way.

If you have read through these two volumes of this *Family Life Handbook* series, you must have seen what the Bible says about divorce. You will also have seen my personal views based on my modest experience of helping couples navigate their marital challenges from a Spirit-led perspective. In stating my biblically-dependent perspectives, I have also done significant research and referenced the work of many leading experts on the subject of family dynamics.

> *While divorce is arguably a very unsettling life event, I believe wholeheartedly that you are still a Christian and you haven't lost your salvation by virtue of your status as a divorced person.*

As a result, I've concluded that divorce is not good and is not approved by the Word of God. However, I still believe that you have not lost your salvation as a divorced person. Romans 8:1 says that there is therefore now no condemnation to those who are in Christ Jesus, who do not walk according to the flesh but according to the Spirit.

THERE IS HOPE AND A FUTURE

This is why I hold the view that a divorced person is still a Christian, and he or she has hope and a beautiful future—both physically and spiritually. I also believe in the possibility that a divorced person can move on and thrive in all spheres of his or her life. But I will reiterate that no Christian should ever be flippant about such a weighty issue as divorce. Make sure that you leave behind a very visible trail of effort you've made to avert divorce before opting for it as a last resort.

Walking in forgiveness as a divorced individual

From a spiritual point of view, it is quite possible that the circumstances that led to your divorce may have caused you to stumble and fall. The experience may probably have shaken your faith in God. As a result, you are no longer walking in the Spirit but in the flesh.

Like many divorced people, you may even have determined in your heart that you will never, ever trust anybody again. I pray that you will pick yourself up, forgive yourself, and forgive your former spouse, as well as anyone else that might have played a role in the failure of your marriage. The Bible says that we should "Pursue peace with all people, and holiness, without which no one will see the Lord" (Hebrews 12:14).

Some divorce experiences have left the couple bruised with deep wounds that will take a very long time to heal. Such wounds usually come from either the perceived or the real cause of the divorce. In many cases, the legal proceedings themselves can be very traumatizing, also leaving the divorcing couple completely drained. Quite often, they are drained physically, spiritually, emotionally, and even financially. That is sometimes called a "bitter divorce experience."

THERE IS HOPE AND A FUTURE

Forgive yourself

How can you possibly forgive others when you are not able to forgive yourself? That is why the first critical step towards your healing journey is to forgive and accept yourself. Self-acceptance is a very important thing to pursue because if you continue to reject yourself, why would you expect others to accept you? In fact, the cloud of self-rejection can sometimes be so thick that it prevents you from seeing the effort others may be making to accept and draw you to themselves. You also need to realize that forgiving yourself is key to being able to forgive your former spouse as well as anyone who may have played a role in your ordeal.

Unfortunately, forgiveness is arguably one of the hardest things anyone will have to do on their journey to finding peace. And for a lot of people, the act of forgiving themselves can be even harder. But what is most important is to discover the overwhelming love of God, which we can always draw from.

> *How can you possibly forgive others when you cannot forgive yourself?*

As a consequence of such an unsettling life event as divorce, one is likely going to sit back, reflect, and come to terms with his or her personal role that contributed to the breakdown of their marriage. As you reflect, perhaps, your most important tool will be the inspiration available from the Word of God, as well as its healing power on anyone that yields to it.

Here are some important inspirational scriptures to feed your spirit with:

THERE IS HOPE AND A FUTURE

The Realm of God's Grace

"… looking carefully lest anyone fall short of the grace of God; lest any root of bitterness springing up cause trouble, and by this many become defiled;" (Hebrews 12:15).

This important scripture tells us that due diligence is required in ensuring that you or your former spouse do not fall short of the grace of God. No matter what the situation might be, strive to be within the realm of the grace of God. You are not safe outside the realm of the grace of God! The grace of God is what you absolutely need to take you through the soul-crushing experience that you might have suffered as part of the divorce process. Also, it is the grace of God that you need to help you get rid of any root of bitterness that typically characterizes the lives of those who have experienced a divorce. That root of bitterness has been known to cause trouble and even the defilement of many.

> *It is the grace of God that you need to help you get rid of any root of bitterness that typically characterizes the lives of those who have experienced a divorce.*

Lean on God's Mercy

"He has not dealt with us according to our sins, Nor punished us according to our iniquities. For as the heavens are high above the earth, So great is His mercy toward those who fear Him" (Psalms 103:10-11).

Whatever role you might have played in the breakdown of your marriage, the Word of God is saying to you that you should stop being so hard on yourself. God is too loving to deal with you according to your failings or limitations as a human being. Being our Maker, he intimately understands our human frailty. The greatness of his mercy can only be compared to the distance between the earth and heaven. Therefore, rejoice you have been forgiven. Quit being so hard on yourself. You will be far better off without the constant self-condemnation.

You're a New Creation

"Therefore, if anyone is in Christ, he is a new creation; old things have passed away; behold, all things have become new" (2 Corinthians 5:17).

You are not the same person who went through a divorce ordeal. Whatever led to it has passed away. You have got to embrace yourself as a brand-new person. That newness includes the physical, spiritual, emotional, and psychological. You are in a new phase of your life that will be more glorious than ever before.

You can't Change your Past

"… but one *thing* I do, forgetting those things which are behind and reaching forward to those things which are ahead" (Philippians 3:13).

Did you know that your life belongs in the future and not in the past? While the past helps us to know where we are coming from; your real focus should be on what lies ahead. Learn from your past experiences and move on! No one can change the events of the past. The best you can do is leverage the past to chart a new course for the future. That's the important message Paul was bringing to the Philippian Christians, that, even in the best of times, it does not help to be living in the fantasies of the past. Therefore, don't allow the unfortunate past to ruin your today and tomorrow.

"Do not be anxious about anything, but in every situation, by prayer and *petition*, with thanksgiving, present your requests to God. And the peace of God, which transcends all understanding, will guard your hearts and your minds in Christ Jesus" (Philippians 4:6-7 NIV).

It is probably superfluous to say that divorce is an experience that can cause anxiety, even in the life of the most psychologically stable, strong, and calm person. However, the Word of God is encouraging you not to give room to anxiety, as anxiety will exacerbate the state of your mind and health, which is probably troubled at this time. Surround yourself with trustworthy prayer support partners as you go through this unpleasant phase of your life.

> ... the Word of God is encouraging you not to give room to anxiety, as anxiety will exacerbate the state of your mind and health, which is probably troubled at this time.

The Bible says that when you do, the benefit that will accrue to you is that the peace of God, which is infinitely beyond what anyone can understand, will watch over your heart and mind to protect or control them from defilement or anything that will have a damaging effect on them. When the peace of God takes over your mind, there will be no room left for unforgiveness, anger, bitterness, or any other such thing to thrive.

THERE IS HOPE AND A FUTURE

I am sure you will be fine with prayers, inspiration from these scriptures (and more), and appropriate social support. However, if you still feel you need to seek some professional therapy, don't hesitate to go for it.

Forgive your Spouse

In Matthew 18:23-35, Jesus taught an important lesson on the act of forgiveness. He said, "For if ye forgive men their trespasses, your Heavenly Father will also forgive you: But if ye forgive not men their trespasses, neither will your Father forgive your trespasses."

Forgive your former spouse for whatever happened that resulted in the failure of your marriage. It will be for your good to forgive him or her. Forgiving them will bring you further healing, peace, and joy. Do your best to avoid the mistake many people make when they carry intense and destructive levels of unforgiveness against somebody, assuming that it will hurt the offender more.

That attitude has been likened to somebody drinking poison while thinking another person will be hurt as a result. No matter the circumstances, you cannot drink poison and expect another person to suffer the consequences. No, the consequences will primarily rest with you. Unforgiveness is toxic, and if you allow it, it'll do irreparable damage to the core of your being.

> *Unforgiveness is toxic, and if you let it, it'll do irreparable damage to the core of your being.*

In addition, if you desire to go into another relationship, forgiveness will prepare you to be emotionally ready for it. You don't want to enter into another relationship full of anger and bitterness. You want to be a happy, joyful, and full-of-life person who has a lot to look forward to in life. That disposition will make you attractive to your next potential partner.

KEY TAKE AWAY

- There is hope and an amazing future for a divorced person.

- A divorced person is still a Christian and he or she can fully fulfill the plan and purpose of God for their lives.

- Don't be too hard on yourself as you work towards putting the unfortunate experience of divorce behind you.

- Bitterness and unforgiveness can potentially render a Christian spiritually ineffective.

- Don't allow your divorce experience to defile your human spirit with the root of bitterness.

- Although, your divorce experience is real, don't let it define you. You have a spectacular future ahead of you. Eagerly look forward to it and leave the past behind you.

- Purging yourself of unforgiveness and bitterness is essential to repositioning yourself physically, spiritually, and emotionally for another relationship.

CHAPTER TWENTY-FOUR

HOPE FOR THE FATHERLESS CHILD

Most probably, you have found out from the preceding pages of this volume that I have joined a coalition of researchers and other godly men and women to advocate that men who, by choice or providence, have become fathers should embrace that task, both in deed and in spirit.

A father should appreciate the fact that his child did not choose to come into this world. You, the father, brought that child into this world. That is one important reason you must stay home and be a father to your child(ren). Your children need you to be truly present in their lives.

That being said, the task of being a father unquestionably comes with challenges in several ways. For example, being a father demands you to be responsible. This is a fact some men are not yet ready to face when becoming fathers. As you provide for your family, fatherhood can also come with additional financial burdens.

However, it should be gratifying to any man to appreciate the importance of being present in the lives of his children. Your presence is not just a luxury for your children. It is a necessity. As documented in Chapter Twenty above, there is abundant empirical evidence that supporting the assertion that children who grow up in the absence of their fathers are often negatively impacted.

> ... there is abundant empirical evidence that supports the assertion that children who grow up in the absence of their fathers are negatively impacted.

For that reason, it will be safe to say that a father who abandons his children with their mom has not done well. However, while the impact of a runaway father on a child can be undeniably significant, let me say here that there is still great hope and a future for that child to grow up to be a successful human being.

Very closely associated with the conundrum of fatherlessness is that there is also the issue of single motherhood. Therefore, if you are a single mother who is raising your children, I want you to know that there is hope and a beautiful future for you and your children. Resist the temptation to be immersed in self-pity. You should also not allow others to pity you. That is not what you need. You should never allow yourself to be defined by the fact that you are a single mom. Instead, be confident and self-assured that all is well with you and your children.

Similarly, do all you can to instill confidence in your children to vehemently reject the label that they are fatherless. They are not fatherless. They just happen to be growing up without a father figure in human form at home. I pray that you will remain physically, emotionally, and psychologically strong for yourself and your children. Above all, remain spiritually strong so you can continue to draw strength to pray and guide your children into a life of greatness.

THERE IS HOPE AND A FUTURE

> *Similarly, do your best to instill confidence in your children to psychologically reject the label that they are fatherless. They are not fatherless. They just happen to be growing up without a father figure in human form around them.*

Certainly, you will never be a father to your beautiful children. But you can be the best mom any child can ever ask for. I have reasons to believe that there is a special place for a mother's prayer in her children's lives. God has shown to be very attentive to a mother who intercedes for her children.

For example, Samuel was born out of the deep groaning of Hannah, his mother, who was known by many as barren. She specifically vowed that if God heard her and blessed her with a son, she would surely give him to the service of the Lord all the days of his life.

> *I have reasons to believe that there is a special place for a mother's prayer in her children's lives.*

And in the fullness of time, God came through in his faithfulness and blessed her with Samuel. And once Samuel was weaned, Hannah fulfilled her vow by giving him to the Lord as a gift. These were her words of testimony as she presented Samuel before Eli: "For this child I prayed; and the Lord has given me my petition which I asked of him. Therefore also, I have lent him to the Lord; as long as he lives he shall be lent to the Lord. And he worshipped the Lord there" (1 Samuel 1:27-28).

THERE IS HOPE AND A FUTURE

As shown in the first book of Samuel, chapter one, it is clear that the circumstances that led to Samuel's birth were legendary. But even more legendary was the way he lived his incredibly illustrious life. Following his dedication to the Lord as a young lad, Samuel exhibited rare poise as a student priest. He was different in every way. He knew that he was in his own class with a special purpose, despite growing up among the lewd sons of Eli. Samuel remained consistently classy in his demeanor even as he continued to enjoy the favor of God and everyone in Israel (1 Samuel 2:26).

Samuel did not deviate from a life of distinction until God eventually chose him as a replacement for Eli and his family, which was designated to be a perpetual lineage of priests. What an honor! The story of the birth and life of Samuel is one of the most beautiful stories in the scriptures. Although Elkanah was present supporting his wife the whole time, the visible role his mother played as an ardent intercessor makes the story of Samuel an unforgettable one. I also believe that it was Hannah's prayers that propelled Samuel to such great success in life and ministry.

> I also believe that it was Hannah's prayers that propelled Samuel to such great success in life and ministry.

Therefore, as a mother of children whom their father has abandoned, you can elect to be that mother who intercedes for her children so they can grow up into adults with superior character and even become models that other children can emulate. You can ensure that your influence on them is so great that their destiny shines like that of Samuel. Yes, it is possible.

THERE IS HOPE AND A FUTURE

You can do it. And may you not ever forget that you can do all things through Christ, who gives you strength (Philippians 4:13).

> *Therefore, as a mother of children whose father has abandoned them, you can elect to be that mother who intercedes for their children so they can grow up into adults with great character and even become models that other children can emulate.*

A word of encouragement for single moms

So, your husband or your children's father has abandoned you with the children. That means you have taken on the role of a single mom. A role you most probably did not prepare for. Like most moms in that situation, you are not a good fit for the role.

To try and grow into it, you're having to work several jobs so you can provide food, shelter, clothing, and other daily essentials for your children. You are working so hard to the point that you have little to no time to be actively involved in the lives of your children the way you would've loved to. Simply expressed, the job of a single mom is clearly over your head! Let me assure you that you are special and highly valued.

In Psalms 34, the Bible says that the Lord is close to the broken hearted and saves those who are crushed in spirit.

Surely, the weight of single motherhood is heavy enough to cause any mom's heart to break and her spirit to be crushed. But the truth of God being up close and the assurance that he'll save you should liven your whole being.

THERE IS HOPE AND A FUTURE

Furthermore, the Word of God says in Jeremiah 29:11, "For I know the thoughts I think towards you, the thoughts of good and not of evil to give you the expected end."

> *You have found an ally, father, provider, and sustainer in God, whose lovingkindness never fails.*

You are not alone; God is close to you, in fact, very close. You are always in God's thoughts. You have found an ally, father, provider, and sustainer in God, whose lovingkindness never fails. I pray that the following Bible verses will bring great comfort and assurance to you as you juggle multiple tasks in your very busy life as a single mother.

How to carve an image of the future for your children

Just in case you haven't done it yet, let me ask you to take a moment, reflect, and start thinking about how and what you want your children to grow into. Let that image be laser-sharp in your mind. The image you have created for your children is the expected end that God has promised to give you. Isn't it refreshing to know that, fortunately, you're not alone in the arduous task of raising your children all by yourself? God has promised to be with you every step of the way until you achieve your desired end for yourself and for your children.

> *Just in case you haven't done it yet, let me ask you to take a moment, reflect, and start thinking about how and what you want your children to grow into.*

THERE IS HOPE AND A FUTURE

The first step in formulating an image for your children's future is to look closely at what the Bible says about them. You have got to see yourself and your children in the light of the Word of God. In other words, you have got to see them the way God sees them.

We learn from Romans 10 that "faith comes by hearing and hearing by the Word of God" (verse 17). Therefore, I'll ask you to make it a habit to declare the appropriate Word of God over your children. You'll note that as you continue to pray the Word of God over your children, you're instilling faith in them. The more they hear it, the more they will be positioned towards becoming what you are speaking into their lives. The word of God is living and will manifest in your children's lives.

> *The more they hear it, the more they will be positioned towards becoming what you are speaking into their lives.*

Here are some fitting Bible verses and a pattern of prayer to declare over your children as routinely as possible:

"A father of the fatherless, a defender of widows, *Is* God in His holy habitation. God sets the solitary in families; He brings out those who are bound into prosperity; But the rebellious dwell in a dry *land*"

(Psalms 69:5-6).

THERE IS HOPE AND A FUTURE

Pray like this:

Father, I thank you for your role as a father of the fatherless. You're also the defender of single mothers like me. Thank you for your never-failing presence around me and my children. You are such a good and faithful Father. You're our provider, defender and protector. With you around us, we feel safe, secure and well-taken care of. Thank you, Lord, for being my defender and the father to my children. You are more than enough. Your name be praised, in Jesus's name, AMEN.

"And his master saw that the Lord was with him and that the Lord made all he did to prosper in his hand. So Joseph found favor in his sight, and served him. Then he made him overseer of his house, and all that he had he put under his authority"

(Genesis 39:2-4).

Pray like this:

In the name of Jesus, I declare that the Lord will be with my children as he was with Joseph. And the Lord will make all that they do to prosper. My children will always find favor in the sight of everyone they come in contact with – those with authority over them as well as their peers. God will cause those lower than you to submit to you and serve you. The favor of God will make you have an excellent spirit so that you can distinguish yourself anywhere you find yourself and get promotions ahead of your peers. People will single you out to show you favor. You will easily find yourself in leadership positions without having to match over others to get to such positions. My children are surrounded by God's favor all-round. In Jesus's name, I pray, AMEN.

THERE IS HOPE AND A FUTURE

"May the Lord God of your fathers make you a thousand times more numerous than you are, and bless you as He has promised you!" (Deuteronomy 1:11).

Pray like this:

In the name of Jesus, I pray that the blessings of God will rest on my children like no one has ever seen before. Whatever they lay hands upon to do is blessed and prosperous. They will not know failure. They will not struggle in life. They are blessed in their going out and in their coming in. Let it be even so in Jesus's Name, I pray, AMEN.

"Now it shall come to pass, if you diligently obey the voice of the Lord your God, to observe carefully all His commandments which I command you today, that the Lord your God will set you high above all nations of the earth. And all these blessings shall come upon you and overtake you, because you obey the voice of the Lord your God:"

"Blessed *shall* you *be* in the city, and blessed *shall* you *be* in the country.

Blessed *shall be* the fruit of your body, the produce of your ground and the increase of your herds, the increase of your cattle and the offspring of your flocks.

Blessed *shall be* your basket and your kneading bowl.

Blessed *shall* you *be* when you come in, and blessed *shall* you *be* when you go out.

THERE IS HOPE AND A FUTURE

The Lord will cause your enemies who rise against you to be defeated before your face; they shall come out against you one way and flee before you seven ways."

(Deuteronomy 28:1-7).

Pray like this:

My children will serve the Lord diligently. They will avoid anything that doesn't give God glory. They will work closely with God all the days of their lives. God will keep them away from harm. They are far removed from ungodly relationships in Jesus name.

God's blessings will follow my children wherever they go. Their going out is blessed and their coming in is also blessed.

They will increase in their financial and material abundance. They will be hugely prosperous.

They will be well-liked anywhere they find themselves. Those who will prefer to be their enemies will be humiliated in defeat in all their schemes. Their enemies will not be able to stand before them at all. If their enemies conspire and come against my children from one direction, the Lord will cause them to be in total disarray, and they will be scattered in seven different directions because of you. In Jesus' name in pray, AMEN.

"Then the Lord your God will give you great success in everything you do. You will have many children. Your livestock will have many little ones. Your crops will do very well. The Lord will take delight in you again. He will give you success…"

(Deuteronomy 30:9 NIRV).

THERE IS HOPE AND A FUTURE

Pray like this:

In the name of Jesus, I declare Deuteronomy 30:9 over my children. My heavenly Father will give you great success in everything you do. In your studies, sports, music classes, work, relationships, and everything else. You will not be associated with failure all the days of your life. Your life will be fruitful, physically, spiritually, materially, and financially. You will grow up to have well-behaved children who will make you proud. Your children will rejoice over you. God will take special delight in you and all that concerns you. You will do exceptionally well in life. In Jesus' Name, I pray, AMEN.

"Though your beginning was small, yet your latter end would increase abundantly."

(Job 8:7).

Pray Like this:

You are growing up without your father. But God is and will always be your father. In the eyes of man, your beginning may look ordinary and small. But the Word of God declares that you are going to grow into a life of greatness and supernatural abundance. You will enjoy a significant increase in the days, weeks, months, and years to come. So shall it be according to God's Word. In Jesus' Name, I pray, AMEN.

"I will praise You, for I am fearfully and wonderfully made; Marvelous are Your works, And that my soul knows very well"

(Psalms 139:14).

THERE IS HOPE AND A FUTURE

Pray Like this:

In the Name of Jesus, I commit to praising you every day of my life. My children and I are fearfully and wonderfully made. Our makeup reflects how great you are as our sovereign Lord who made the heavens and earth. My children and I are the work of your hands and marvelous are your works. I know it. My children also know just how awesome and wonderfully made they are. We thank you, Lord, for everything! In Jesus' Name, I pray, AMEN.

"Riches and honor are with me, Enduring riches and righteousness"

(Proverbs 8:18).

Pray like this:

Father, I thank you for blessing me and my children with so many riches and honor. We're flourishing in every area of our lives as a family. We're wealthy. You have also clothed us with honor. We have everything we need because you are our provider. And we'll always have all our needs met because we serve a faithful God whose love and mercy endure forever. My children and I thank you, Lord, so much for your lovingkindness. In Jesus' Name, I pray, AMEN.

"Here am I and the children whom the Lord has given me! We are for signs and wonders …"

(Isaiah 8:18).

THERE IS HOPE AND A FUTURE

Pray like this:

Father, I thank you for the gift of children. You have blessed me with the best children that any parent can ever ask for. I am so proud of them as a gift from you. We are dwelling under the shadow of your wings. You are our shield and our buckler. We stand on your Word that says that we are for signs and wonders in the land of the living. Anyone that knows us knows that our lives praise, honor, and magnify you. Your daily provisions are a clear testament that our home is your dwelling place because there can't be any lack where you dwell. How can we thank you enough for all that you have bestowed on us? We will praise you as a family all the days of our lives. Thank you, Lord. In Jesus' Name, I pray, AMEN.

"Blessed be the God and Father of our Lord Jesus Christ, who has blessed us with every spiritual blessing in the heavenly places in Christ, just as He chose us in Him before the foundation of the world, that we should be holy and without blame before Him in love, having predestined us to adoption as sons by Jesus Christ to Himself, according to the good pleasure of His will, to the praise of the glory of His grace, by which He made us accepted in the Beloved"

(Ephesians 1:3-6).

Pray like this:

Father, you have blessed us with every spiritual blessing in the heavenly places in Christ Jesus. We thank you so much for these blessings. You've chosen us to be called your very own, even when we're most undeserving. You've adopted us as sons and daughters through Christ Jesus. You've made us your children, which means we can proudly call you our father. Yes, you're the father of my children. You've accepted us, which is what really matters. Thank you for adopting us and giving us a special place in your kingdom. Your acceptance of us nullifies any rejection that is out there in this world. This revelation gives us so much joy, hope, comfort, and assurance. We thank you, Lord. In Jesus' Name, I pray, Amen.

"I can do all things through Christ who strengthens me."

(Philippians 4:13).

Pray like this:

Lord, I thank you for the strength which you give me every day. With your great strength that is available to me, I am sure that your sufficiency is ours. Your strength gives us the capacity to do anything our hearts desire. In you, there is absolutely nothing we cannot achieve. My children are capable because your strength is available to them in an unlimited measure. Lord, you are so good, and I praise you forevermore. In Jesus' name, I pray, Amen.

"… and you are complete in Him, who is the head of all principality and power"

(Colossians 2:10).

Pray like this:

In the name of Jesus, thank you for the completeness that we have attained because we belong to you. Yes, my children are complete in you, O Lord. For being yours has earned our completeness. Being in you means we lack absolutely nothing. We are not inadequate in any way. We are well-rounded and complete in you. Because my children are complete in you, the absence of their father in our lives makes no difference. You have surrounded us with your goodness and lovingkindness. Thank you, Lord. In Jesus' Name, I pray, Amen.

One more way a single mom can position her children for a great future is to look around and see if there is a family with similar circumstances to you that is exceptional. You can use such a family to model your children. You can assure them that God is on your side as you raise them, and nothing whatsoever is going to cause a limitation to the fulfillment of their destiny. You may point out some examples of those who grew up without their fathers but have excelled in becoming spiritual, political, business, professional, or community leaders.

Such words of affirmation will go a long way in instilling an iron-clad resolve and confidence in them. Therefore, let that image be crystal clear in your mind. Help them embrace and own that image as theirs and watch them grow into a life of greatness and excellence. That image will help organize your life and guide you to what's important and where you need to channel your energy.

Do not be shy about setting a high bar for your children. Remember that the bar you set for them early on will be key to determining the trajectory of their lives. A low bar means that they shouldn't think well about themselves and what they are capable of accomplishing. On the other hand, a high bar means that you are instilling an "I can do" mentality in them, which gives them the confidence to always remain conscious of doing well in life.

THERE IS HOPE AND A FUTURE

> On the other hand, a high bar means that you are instilling an "I can do" mentality in them, which gives them the confidence to always remain conscious of doing well in life.

Perhaps you are a young person growing up without your father. I would like to assure you that you have a future and a beautiful hope. For sure, the absence of your father is an important factor. However, I pray that you will grow up to fulfill your full potential and destiny. To fulfill your destiny, believe what the Word of God says about you. In addition, I will also counsel you to look at the lives of children who grew up with or without their fathers and have turned out to be noteworthy individuals.

KEY TAKE AWAY

- The hole that fatherlessness often creates in the lives in children can be sealed by looking up to and trusting God wholeheartedly.

- The child without a father figure can still thrive and grow up to become a very successful individual.

- The single mom can never become a father to her children. But she can be the best mom that any child can ever ask for.

- The prayer of a praying mom has a special place in the heart of God in turning things around for her children.

- A praying mom can carve an image of what her children will grow up to be, and God shows his faithfulness in bringing them to that expected end.

- A praying mom instils faith, confidence, courage, and assurance in her children by declaring the appropriate scriptures over them every day.

- Carefully select role models from both those who grew up with or without a father.

End Notes for Chapter Twenty Four

1. Judith Wallerstein, et al., The Unexpected Legacy of Divorce: A 25 Year Landmark Study, (New York: Hyperion, 2000), p. xxvii.; Catherine E. Ross and John Mirowsky. "Parental Divorce, Life-Course Disruption, and Adult Depression.," Journal of Marriage and the Family 61 (1999): 1034-1035.

2. Wallerstein, et al., 2000, p. xxix.

3. Andrew J. Cherlin, P. Lindsey Chase-Lansdale and C. McRae, «Effects of Parental Divorce on Mental Health Through the Life Course," American Sociological Review, 63 (1998): 239-249; Catherine E. Ross and John Mirowsky, "Parental Divorce, Life-Course Disruption, and Adult Depression," Journal of Marriage and the Family 61 (1999): 1034-1035.

4. William G. Axinn and Arland Thornton, "The Influence of Parents' Marital Dissolutions on Children's Attitudes toward Family Formation," Demography 33 (1996): 66-81.

5. Glenn T. Stanton, Why Marriage Matters: Reasons to Believe in Marriage in Postmodern Society (Colorado Springs: Pinon Press, 1997), p. 55-70; David Popenoe and Barbara Dafoe Whitehead, «Should We Live Together?» a report of the National Marriage Project, 1999, http://marriage.rutgers.edu.

6. Alan Booth and David Johnson, «Premarital Cohabitation and Marital Success,» Journal of Family Issues 9 (1988): 255-272; Paul Amato and Alan Booth, «The Consequences of Divorce for Attitudes toward Divorce and Gender Roles,» Journal of Family Issues 12 (1991): 306-323.

7   Jane Meredith Adams «Judith Wallerstein: Forget the Notion Divorce Won›t Hurt Kids. It Will,» Biography 1 (1997): 79-81.

8   Wallerstein, et al., 2000, p. xxix.

9   Interview with Steven Earll, M.A., M.S., L.P.C., C.A.C. III, August

10 Fagan, P., & Rector, R. (2000, June 5). *The effects of divorce on America*. The Heritage Foundation. Retrieved April 16, 2022, from https://www.heritage.org/marriage-and-family/report/the-effects-divorce-america

11 Lexico Dictionaries. (n.d.). *Nourish: Meaning & definition for UK English*. Lexico Dictionaries | English. Retrieved April 15, 2022, from https://www.lexico.com/definition/nourish

12 SAMHSA. (n.d.). *Learn the eight dimensions of wellness - store.samhsa.gov*. store.samhsa.gov. Retrieved April 15, 2022, from http://www.store.samhsa.gov/sites/default/files/d7/priv/sma16-4953.pdf

13 Carson, D. A. (2015). *The Pillar New Testament Commentary*, *6*(1), 121. https://doi.org/10.1628/186870315x14249562918073

14 Winch, G. (2014). In *Emotional First Aid: Healing rejection, guilt, failure, and other everyday hurts*. essay, Penguin.

[15] *The Effects of Divorce on America.* Biblical Counseling Coalition. (n.d.). Retrieved April 16, 2022, from https://www.biblicalcounselingcoalition.org/wp-content/uploads/2018/04/The-Effects-of-Divorce-on-America.pdf

[16] Denise French, C. V. A. (2021, May 18). *Why Second marriages Fail.* Divorce Strategies Group. Retrieved April 16, 2022, from https://divorcestrategiesgroup.com/why-second-marriages-fail/

[17] Fagan, P., & Rector, R. (2000, June 5). *The effects of divorce on America.* The Heritage Foundation. Retrieved April 15, 2022, from https://www.heritage.org/marriage-and-family/report/the-effects-divorce-america

[18] Fagan, P. (n.d.). *The real root causes of violent crime: The breakdown of marriage, family, and community.* The Heritage Foundation. Retrieved April 16, 2022, from https://www.heritage.org/crime-and-justice/report/the-real-root-causes-violent-crime-the-breakdown-marriage-family-and

ABOUT THE AUTHOR

Mannie is a second-generation minister of the gospel of Jesus Christ. He's the founding pastor at Kings' Christian Center (a.k.a. Royal Gateway Church) Calgary. He loves the Word, which he teaches with infectious passion and conviction.

Mannie has been happily married to his friend, Dr. Chino, for over 25 years. He's a marriage counsellor, Bible teacher, author, and intercessor. He's widely known for his love for family and the institution of marriage. Mannie's burning desire is to see Kings' Christian Center become a destination of choice for strengthening marriages.

His other published titles include: Dating Etiquette for Singles, The Dynamics of Godly Success, and The Greatest Exchange

CPSIA information can be obtained
at www.ICGtesting.com
Printed in the USA
BVHW041450141022
649461BV00018B/1182/J